Unforgotten

LESSONS FROM LESSER-KNOWN
WOMEN OF THE BIBLE
ON LEAVING A LEGACY OF FAITH

AMG
PUBLISHERS

LEIGH POWERS

Following God

UNFORGOTTEN: LESSONS FROM LESSER-KNOWN WOMEN OF THE BIBLE ON LEAVING A LEGACY OF FAITH

Published by AMG Publishers. All Rights Reserved.

ISBN 13: 978-1-61715-533-8

Manuscript editing, text design, and layout by Rick Steele Editorial Services
http://steeleeditorialservices.myportfolio.com

Cover illustration by Daryle Beam/Bright Boy Design

Printed in the United States of America
2022 First Edition

For my mother and all those who left a legacy of faith for me.

Leigh Powers

LEIGH POWERS has had a lifelong love affair with the Word of God. A pastor's wife, mother of three, speaker, and award-winning author, she has published over three hundred Bible study lessons and devotions and strives to combine solid biblical study with real-world application. She is passionate about helping women find their places in God's great story of salvation.

Leigh is a graduate of Baylor University and Southwestern Baptist Theological Seminary and has twenty years of ministry experience. In addition to serving alongside her husband in the local church, she has also served as a collegiate minister and led outreach to international students. As a high school English teacher, she spends her days helping students fall in love with books and discover the courage to tell their own stories.

Leigh and her family make their home in the greater Houston area. You can usually find her with either a book or knitting needles in her hand—and sometimes both.

I made the library my first stop when I arrived on campus. A helpful assistant obliged me by pulling student directories from the 1940s out of the archives, and I paged through them until I found my grandmother's name. She was listed as a student in the School of Education, a member of only the second class of women to enter the seminary.

I hadn't chosen the school solely because my grandfather and grandmother had attended there, but I liked the feeling of walking in their footsteps. After my grandmother passed away, my aunt found a note one of her professors had scrawled across an old term paper. He thanked her for her academic excellence and said she would "open doors through which other women could follow." As I walked down the sidewalk beneath the arched branches of the pecan trees, I knew I was benefiting from her legacy.

I've reflected on my grandmother's legacy over the years. Grandma never wrote any books or held any significant office. She lived out her life and ministry as a small-town pastor's wife, spending many years as my grandfather's unpaid minister of education and discipleship. She was simply faithful. I can see her legacy of faith written across the generations of our family tree. It's a heritage I'm proud to receive.

Something about our digital world makes us hungry to leave that kind of legacy—a legacy that says we made an impact on this world. The hunger for meaning and connection is one of the top needs identified by millennials, but that drive isn't unique only to the generation born between 1980 and 1994. Regardless of when or where we were born, we hunger for meaning and purpose.

Our craving for meaning came home to me several years ago as I led a small group Bible study for a group of teenage girls. That evening we were talking about our goals and purpose, and I asked the girls to think about what they really wanted in life. They all chimed in and visited about their answers—all except Jessie, who sat slouching in the corner of the room. Jessie came more because her parents made her come than because she wanted to be there, and she made it her mission every week to let everyone in the room know as clearly as possible how little she wanted to be there. That night she suddenly sat up and lifted her chin off her knees as she spoke.

"You know what I want?" she said. "I want to matter."

The girls all nodded. They wanted the same thing—and so did I. Most of us do. We want to matter. We want to make a difference in such a way that the generations to come know we have truly lived.

As we look through the pages of Scripture, we find the stories of women who left a legacy of faith. Women like Esther, who risked her life to save her people. Women like Ruth, whose extraordinary compassion and faithfulness earned her a place in Jesus's family tree. Women like Eve, whose greatest failure brought sin into the world but who also paved the way for our greatest salvation.

We know their stories, but as we read the chronicles of their lives, we might wonder where we fit in this great story of salvation God is telling. Where do I belong if I'm not a Persian queen, the first woman who ever lived, or a great-grandmother of Israel's greatest king? What if life is just normal? No great national crisis, no monumental moment of decision and courage—only daily choices of faithful obedience that lead to a life well lived? Are legacies only for the great heroes of faith, or can they also be for me?

The good news about legacies is that they come in all shapes and sizes. Legacies aren't just for the people whose names get written down in the history books or leave their marks on the Hollywood Walk of Fame. Your legacy isn't determined by how many followers you have on Twitter or likes you have on Instagram. Your legacy is shaped by being faithful to the calling and the purpose God created you for—a purpose ordained for you before the foundation of the world.

Reading Scripture can be like looking at the stars. One of my favorite things to do when we camp is lie in our hammock and gaze up at a night sky unpolluted by street lights and city glare. At first all I see are the same familiar constellations, but as my eyes adjust, I start to see more. The night sky reveals a galaxy of stars that are always there, but which I don't recognize until I take the time to really see.

In the same way, a quick glance at Scripture reveals the same familiar stories we've heard before. But when we slow down to and take the time to look, other stories start to stand out to us—stories of women who played a role in God's great story of salvation. Not all of them are named. Some of them are only mentioned in a line or a phrase, but they were significant enough for their stories to be recorded in the Book of Life. By studying them, we can learn for ourselves what it means to live a legacy of faith—what it looks like to live a life that is worthy of being remembered.

Over the next few weeks, we're going to study the stories of six of these lesser-known women of the Bible. None of them had much time in the spotlight. They are the supporting cast—the roles that get listed way down in the credits right before the makeup artists and the lighting crew. Yet they are woven into the tapestry of faith, and we should consider their stories significant because God says they are significant to him.

Consider:

- The five daughters of Zelophehad, who courageously claimed their inheritance.

- Huldah, who valued God's Word and helped usher in revival.

- Abigail, whose words averted disaster and helped call King David into his destiny.

- The Widow of Zarephath, who wasn't searching for God but discovered God was searching for her.

- Leah, the unloved sister who found acceptance in God's presence and purpose

- Gomer, who discovered the power of God's redeeming love.

- They aren't the women of the Bible whose names always make the Sunday School list, but their lives mattered. Their stories matter.

So does yours.

LEIGH POWERS

Contents

LESSON 1

DAUGHTERS OF ZELOPHEHAD
CLAIMING YOUR INHERITANCE

DAY ONE

A TALE OF FIVE SISTERS

Pieces of our family history are scattered throughout our home. The wardrobe my husband uses is the first piece of furniture his grandparents bought after they got married. A glass peanut jar that belonged to my father's brother sits on top of my kitchen cabinets next to a couple pieces of my grandmother's china and a vase I picked up on a trip to Thailand. Our rock garden is the home for quartz crystals and pieces of petrified wood my rockhound children have collected on family adventures. Our home tells our family's story.

The daughters of Zelophehad found their family story at risk. We find their story in the book of Numbers—a book that is all about transitions. Numbers tells the story of how the Hebrew people came to the edge of the promised land and refused to enter because they feared the giants in the land. Because of their lack of faith, God said the Hebrew people would wander in the wilderness until that entire unfaithful generation had passed away. The rest of the book deals with the transition between the first generation and the second. The final chapters see the new generation making plans to finally enter the promised land. They discuss how they are to live in the land God had promised them and how they will divide the land up among the twelve tribes.

That's where the daughters of Zelophehad come in.

Their story is not one that we tell often, but a few details about the story tell us we should grab our highlighters and perk up our ears. For one thing, all five women are named: Mahlah, Noah, Hoglah, Milcah, and Tirzah. In a time when women often were not named in Scripture, the fact that Numbers lists all five of their names lets us know that the Israelites believed they were worthy of remembering. Secondly, Scripture returns to their story multiple times—mentioning them three times in Numbers as well as in Joshua and 1 Chronicles. What made their legacy meaningful enough for them to be mentioned in Scripture not just once but five times? What does their legacy mean for us?

Mahlah, Noah, Hoglah, Milcah, and Tirzah were five daughters of a man from the tribe of Manesseh named Zelophehad. He died in the wilderness along with the rest of the generation who had left Egypt, but he had no sons to carry on the family name. As Israel began to discuss how they would divide the land, the daughters of Zelophehad realized that their future was at risk. Courageously, the five women brought their case directly to Moses at the entrance of the tent of meeting. The tent of meeting was another name for the tabernacle (Exodus 40:2) and was the place where the people met with God. By coming there, the daughters were bringing their case to God Himself—and God heard their plea.

📖 Read Numbers 27:1-11.

 DID YOU KNOW?
Korah's Rebellion

Korah led a rebellion against Moses's and Aaron's leadership (Numbers 26:8–11). He died because of his rebellion against God, but his line did not die out. If the line of a man who had rebelled against God was preserved, the daughters of Zelophehad thought their father's legacy should also be preserved.

What problem do the daughters of Zelophehad bring before the Lord? What was at stake for them?

_____

_____

_____

_____

How does the Lord respond?

_____

_____

Based on this passage, how does God's response to these women set a precedent for the future?

_____

_____

_____

The case of the daughters of Zelophehad established an important legal precedent for Israel. The nations surrounding Israel allowed women to inherit in some cases, but there is a wide variety of examples of how female inheritance was handled. Dr. Zafira Ben Barak, an expert on Ancient Near Eastern history, conducted a extensive review of inheritance in the ancient world. Through a study of documents left in cities across Mesopotamia, Ben Barak found that women did inherit from their fathers, but how this inheritance was handled was at the father's discretion. Even when Ben Barak studied wills found in a single location such as Nuzi, she found that these wills failed to follow any unified set of principles for inheritance. For example, one ancient will describes how a father adopted a son rather than leave his inheritance to his daughter. In another, the parents pass over a married daughter to leave their inheritance to a single daughter, and others simply divide the inheritance among the daughters. The ability for women to inherit and the conditions under which they were able to inherit were subject to the whims of their families and communities. Having a legal precedent that established rules of female inheritance as codified law and protected women's right to inherit set Israel apart from their neighbors.[1]

The financial security of their father's inheritance was important, but more was at stake for the daughters of Zelophehad than inheriting a small plot of land in Canaan. For Israel, the land was more than just a place to grow figs and wheat. The land was the fulfillment of God's promise and proof that those who possessed it were members of God's chosen people.

📖 Read Deuteronomy 1:8.

To whom does God promise the land?

_____

📖 Read Deuteronomy 4:1 and 4:40.

What is the condition by which the people would possess the land?

_____

📖 Read Joshua 23:16.

What would happen if the people broke their covenant promises to God?

_____

Israel understood that the land belonged to God. As they saw it, Israel was not taking the land; God, the rightful owner of the land, was giving it to His people. The land symbolized God's covenant—God's solemn and unbreakable promise—with His people. Each family received a share of the land and the assurance of God's protection and care.[2] Since Zelophehad had died without sons, there was no one to carry on his family name, meaning he would be forgotten by the generations to come. His daughters were also in a vulnerable position. As unmarried women who had no brothers who could inherit and share the land with them, their options for providing for themselves were limited. Were they still members of the covenant community? Did God's promises apply to them?

The five sisters showed faith in bringing their concern before the Lord. Their circumstances were less than ideal. Yet the daughters determined to show faith in God's promise despite their circumstances. They were looking for God to validate their claim and give them the means to provide for themselves, but they were also asking God to validate them as members of God's covenant community.

God did. God's word to Moses was that what the daughters of Zelophehad were saying was "right." The Hebrew word means "straight" or "honest." They spoke correctly—and understood God correctly. The heart of the covenant was God's relationship with His people. Faith in God's promise and obedience to God's commands were what kept the covenant in effect. While the first generation who left Egypt was marked by defiance and unbelief, the daughters of Zelophehad demonstrated courageous faith in our promise-keeping God. They stood before Moses and the entire congregation of Israel to ask God to keep His promises to them.

God did.

Have you ever wondered if God's promises apply to you? Why?

_____

_____

_____

How have circumstances tested your faith? How did you respond?

_____

_____

_____

When circumstances test our faith, how can we show courageous belief in our promise keeping God?

_____

_____

_____

DAY TWO

LIFE ON THE BOUNDARY LINES

One of the reasons this moment was so significant for the daughters of Zelophehad was that they were living in an uncertain position in the Israelite community. Their crisis created an opportunity to reveal something vital about the character of God.

As women with no male relative to provide for them, the daughters of Zelophehad were in a vulnerable position. They had no father to negotiate marriage contracts for them or protect them from exploitation. Their options for earning a living were limited. Beyond that, their place in Israel's social fabric was at stake. In a world where women typically went directly from the home of their father to the home of their husband, a group of women on their own didn't quite fit into the community.

Liminality is a word that describes life at times of transition. To be liminal is to live at the boundaries, experiencing the uncertainty of not being fully one thing or another. When they lost their father, the daughters of Zelophehad took up a liminal position. They were not daughters under a father's protection. They were not wives living in their husband's household. They were not widows being cared for by their own children. They didn't fit any of the categories the people of Israel normally assigned to women, and that placed them on the boundaries of society.

Have you ever been in a situation where you lived on the boundaries? A place where you didn't quite fit? What was that like? How did it feel?

Given their precarious position, we might excuse the daughters if they took the easy path of marrying the first man who would have them or becoming servants in someone else's household. This route would have meant letting their father's name and legacy pass into oblivion—something faithful Israelites considered deeply shameful. Instead, Zelophehad's daughters took the harder route of forging new ground.

DID YOU KNOW?
A Disappearing Name

"Why should our father's name disappear from his clan because he had no son?" (Numbers 27:4). For a name to "disappear" meant that it was dropped from Israel's genealogical records because the father had no sons to carry on his name. A man's name disappearing was often a result of God's judgment. This association led to the belief that it was shameful for a family name to disappear.

Read Numbers 27:4 again. Keeping in mind the daughters' position at the boundary of society, what were they asking Moses to do for them?

By asking that their father's name not be forgotten, the daughters were also asking that they not be forgotten. They weren't content to live on the fringes as outsiders looking in. They believed that their father's death had not made them lesser members of God's people, consigned to be onlookers while others received the fullness of God's promise. They believed that God's promises were vast enough and powerful enough to include them, and they put their faith into action by asking God to remember them in the presence of all the people.

God did. This should not surprise us. Throughout the Old Testament, we see that God has a special concern for those who live on the fringes of society. God is the protector of the vulnerable and transforms those who live on the borders into valued members of society. God calls Himself the "father of the fatherless, a defender of widows" (Psalm 68:5). In the Hebrew law, God told the people that anyone who perverted the justice due to the sojourner, the fatherless, or the widow, would be cursed (Deuteronomy 27:5). God also decreed that "you, your sons and daughters, your male and female servants, the Levites in your towns, and the foreigners, the fatherless and the widows living among you" should celebrate at Israel's appointed festivals (Deuteronomy 16:11). Israel was not to limit membership among the people of God to the landowners and the wealthy. Slaves, foreigners, widows, and orphans—all the most vulnerable members of society—were meant to be included in the celebration.

God continues the same pattern in the New Testament. Jesus ate and drank with the tax collectors and sinners, ignoring the complaints of the religious leaders who said such company was inappropriate for a rabbi. He crossed religious and ethnic boundaries to show God's grace to a Samaritan woman who lived on the fringes of her own community, transforming her from outcast to emissary. He touched lepers and refused to flinch away from a sinful woman who washed His feet with her own hair. Jesus healed the servant of a Roman centurion and the daughter of a Canaanite woman. He made it clear that God's love and grace reached to all people—including those who live on the fringes of society.

It should not surprise us that God continued this pattern of taking those on the fringes and transforming them into integral members of the community in the church.

Read Galatians 3:28–29 and write these verses out below:

_____

_____

_____

_____

Roman society was rigidly stratified into social groups. The believers who first read Paul's letter to the church at Galatia would have instantly recognized the deep social chasms that existed between Jews and Greeks, men and women, and slaves and free people. Yet God said that in the church, none of this system of social ranking and power should have any meaning. All stood in need of Christ's grace, and all who received Christ were now members of the community of faith—children of Abraham and heirs of God.

We need this message today. We may not group ourselves into groups of Jew and Greek or slave and free, but we still splinter into our own factions and groups. We divide between rich and poor, black and white, liberal and conservative, people who watch *Fixer Upper* and people who watch *Game of Thrones*. Yet God still declares that our definitions and separations lose their significance under Christ's banner. God takes those on the fringes and brings them into the center of the community.

📖 Reread Galatians 3:28–29. How could you rewrite this verse using ways we separate ourselves today?

"There is neither _____ nor _____, neither _____ nor _____, nor is there _____ and _____, for you are all one in Christ Jesus. If you belong to Christ, then you are Abraham's seed, and heirs according to the promise."

Read that last part again: "If you belong to Christ, then you are Abraham's seed, and heirs according to the promise." If you have asked God to forgive you of your sins and followed Him as Lord, than you stand next to the daughters of Zelophehad as Abraham's descendants, heirs according to the promise of God.

I want you to hear this: you belong. God did not save you to leave you on the sidelines. Your past does not exclude you from God's promises. The amount of money in your bank or amount of gray in your hair does not push you out of the circle. The color of your skin does not determine the value of your character. If you are married or single, career woman or stay at home mom, the kind of woman who likes to bake or the kind of woman who builds a ninja course in her backyard, you have a place among God's people. More than a place—God values you. God treasures you. And God says you are His.

You don't have to live a liminal life. Jesus has already welcomed you in.

DAY THREE

OUR PLACE TO BELONG

We've seen already that the request that the five daughters of Zelophehad brought before the Lord was about more than just a few acres of farmland. The core of their question is an issue of belonging: Did they as five single women truly belong as equals among God's people? God said that they did. It is this declaration that makes their story so significant that these five sisters are mentioned five times in Scripture.

How do we apply this story to our lives as women living in the twenty-first century? We can find our place of belonging in the same place the daughters of Zelophehad did—among the community of God's people.

There are differences, of course. We are not citizens of the nation of Israel. Today, the community of faith is not defined by common ancestry but through a common experience of salvation in Jesus Christ. The community in which we celebrate our belonging is known as the local church.

I'll be the first to admit that we get this church thing wrong sometimes. We Christians often fail to be the welcoming people of God we are meant to be. I've experienced it. After a cross-country move, I started looking for a church in my new town. I showed up at one church during a midweek Bible study and found a seat in the back. No one spoke to me. Now, I'm quiet—I'll admit to that. I'm not the kind to stand up in a crowd and shout, "Here I am!" Even so, this group was small enough that it should have been obvious that I was a visitor. No one spoke to me or sat by me before, during, or after the meeting. I left after the study was over without anyone so much as acknowledging I was in the room. When I got outside, I discovered that someone had written WASH ME in all capital letters in the dust on the trunk of my car.

I didn't feel I belonged that day. I left feeling unwanted, unwelcome, and alone. I eventually found a wonderful church in my new hometown, but that experience taught me to keep an eye out for visitors to our congregation.

Yet I am reminded that while we sometimes fail to be the people of God we are meant to be, our failures do not have to limit our possibilities. Several years later my husband and I visited another church for the first time. We didn't expect to wind up making it our church home, but we were new in town and could see the steeple from our apartment.

How different that experience was from my lonely night several years before! People greeted us at the door and invited us to sit next to them. They went out of their way to shake our hands during the greeting time. The pastor introduced himself. The young adult class invited us to a baked potato supper at a church member's home after the service. Before we knew it, we were in this couple's home eating baked potatoes and laughing with people who had been strangers to us an hour ago. Both my husband and I knew that night that we had found our church home. We were strangers, but they showed us God's heart for welcoming the stranger in.

God's desire is still to rescue those who are far off from Him and give them a place to belong.

📖 Read Ephesians 2:11–22.

What groups were far off and apart from Christ? How did God bring those groups near?

_____

_____

_____

What words or phrases in this passage speak to God's desire to give us a place to belong?

_____

Where do we find our place to belong?

Paul wrote Ephesians to a church grappling with the ethnic divisions between Jews and Gentiles, or non-Jews. The Jews understood themselves to be God's chosen people, the only nation on earth worthy of receiving God's law and favor. After Christ's resurrection, His primarily Jewish followers had to undergo a paradigm shift. God's heart had always been to redeem all peoples, but it took time for the early church to understand this. As they began reaching out to non-Jews, many Gentiles eagerly embraced Christ and came into the church. This created a problem for Jewish believers: Did these non-Jewish followers of Christ have to become Jewish in order to become Christians? In other words, did they have to follow the Jewish law in order to follow Christ?

Paul's emphatic answer to this question was "No!" Paul understood that we are saved by grace alone. In passages like this one in Ephesians, Paul underscored how both Jews and Gentiles were now one in Christ. Through Christ's sacrifice, God had torn down the dividing wall between Jews and non-Jews and created something new: a united church. Through the Spirit of God, all who called on the name of Christ now had access to the Father regardless of their ancestry or ethnicity. They were no longer "foreigners and strangers," but "fellow citizens with God's people and also members of his household" (Ephesians 2:19). Together God was building them into something new: a temple not built from bricks and stone but from the hearts of all those who call on the name of the Lord. In the Old Testament God dwelt in the tabernacle and the temple. Today the Holy Spirit dwells in the hearts of men and women who follow Jesus Christ as Lord. Together, we are the temple of God—the place where God dwells and where God is worshiped.

📖 Reread verses 19–22 again. How do these verses describe the church? What does that description imply about the importance of worshiping together with the people of God?

Our participation in a local community of believers is vital to our walk with Christ. When we gather together as God's people, we are something greater than the sum of our parts. Together we form a faith community that hosts the person, presence, and power of the Spirit of God. Removing ourselves from that community means the church misses out on the opportunity to experience God working in and through us and that we miss the opportunity to hear the voice of God speaking through His people. Our presence is vital.

The church is meant to be a place where we are welcomed, and it is also meant to be a place where together we welcome God.

We are a redeemed people, not a perfect people. We do not always live up to who God has created us to be. Yet God works in and through us, continuing to tear down the walls that divide us and bring us to Him.

Over the years I've met many people who carry the scars of church pain. Sometimes this pain drives people from the church—they love Jesus but can't stomach walking through the church doors again. Other people fear walking through the doors of the church because they believe they'll find a place of condemnation instead of hope—that church people will look at their tattoos or their scars or the dirt on the trunk of their car and find a reason to turn their back. If this is you, know God has created a place for you to belong. Like the daughters of Zelophehad, take courage. Step forward and keep searching until you find it.

Maybe you find yourself in a different place. Maybe like me you toddled through the church doors, or you've been a part of your congregation for so long that you've forgotten how unfamiliar it can feel to people who don't know the words to the songs or when to stand and sit at the right time. Keep your eyes open. Know that any given Sunday, someone will walk through the doors of your church who feels a little unsure. Someone who may fumble to find the right page in her Bible, doesn't know where the bathrooms are, and who is wondering if this can be a place where she fits in. Find her. Save her a seat. And answer her unspoken question. *Yes, you belong. You belong here.*

Have you found a place to belong in the community of God's people? If yes, how has this experience blessed you? If not, what is one action you can take this week to find your place to belong?

DAY FOUR

CLAIMING OUR INHERITANCE

The five daughters of Zelophehad stepped forward to claim their inheritance. As we've seen, for Israel, inheritance was about more than just the land. It encompassed their status as God's people. Inheriting the land symbolized both that God claimed Israel as His inheritance and the Lord was Israel's inheritance. For the daughters of Zelophehad, claiming their inheritance had to do with their relationship with God.

What does it mean for us to claim our inheritance? As believers in Christ, do we have an inheritance? What is it? And what difference does that inheritance make in our lives?

The theme of inheritance flows through the New Testament. Inheritance language such as *heir, inheritance, inherit,* and so on, is used sixty-five times in the New Testament. While a few of these usages refer to the transfer of property from father to son, the vast majority of these occurrences have to do with the eternal inheritance Christ has secured for us.[3] Consider the following passages:

> *For this reason Christ is the mediator of a new covenant, that those who are called may receive the promised eternal inheritance—now that he has died as a ransom to set them free from the sins committed under the first covenant. (Hebrews 9:15)*

> *Praise be to the God and Father of our Lord Jesus Christ! In his great mercy he has given us new birth into a living hope through the resurrection of Jesus Christ from the dead, and into an inheritance that can never perish, spoil or fade. This inheritance is kept in heaven for you, who through faith are shielded by God's power until the coming of the salvation that is ready to be revealed in the last time. (1 Peter 1:3-5)*

> *Now if we are children, then we are heirs—heirs of God and co-heirs with Christ, if indeed we share in his sufferings in order that we may also share in his glory. (Romans 8:17)*

📖 Reread the previous passages and underline the words *heir* or *inheritance* in each verse. What do these verses teach us about our inheritance in Christ?

_____

_____

_____

_____

There are five characteristics of inheritance in the New Testament.

1. Christ is the heir of all things.

> *...in these last days he has spoken to us by his Son, whom he appointed heir of all things, and through whom also he made the universe. (Hebrews 1:2)*

God has named Jesus His heir over all creation. The cosmos is His twice over. The universe was made through Christ and redeemed through His sacrifice. Because he is God's son, Creator, and Redeemer, God has appointed Jesus heir of all things.

2. We are joint heirs with Christ because we have been adopted as God's children.

> *In love he predestined us for adoption to sonship through Jesus*
> *Christ, in accordance with his pleasure and will. (Ephesians 1:4b–5)*

> *If you belong to Christ, then you are Abraham's seed, and heirs*
> *according to the promise" (Galatians 3:29)*

We are God's children not by birth but by adoption. Though we were strangers to God, God made us part of His own household. We now share in Christ's inheritance.

3. Our inheritance is a gift of God's grace.

> *It was not through the law that Abraham and his offspring received*
> *the promise that he would be heir of the world, but through the*
> *righteousness that comes by faith. For if those who depend on the*
> *law are heirs, faith means nothing and the promise is worth-*
> *less. . . . (Romans 4:13–15)*

By its very nature, an inheritance is something received, not earned. When we receive an inheritance, we benefit from someone else's labor. In the same way, our inheritance in Christ is a gift of God's grace. It comes by God's promise through faith, not our own effort or works.

4. Our inheritance includes the blessings and benefits of our relationship with Christ and life in the kingdom of God.

Israel inherited the land. We inherit the kingdom, and God lavishes His blessings upon us.

> *In him we have redemption through his blood, the forgiveness of sins,*
> *in accordance with the riches of God's grace that he lavished on us.*
> *(Ephesians 1:7–8)*

> *. . . giving joyful thanks to the Father, who has qualified you to*
> *share in the inheritance of his holy people in the kingdom of light.*
> *(Colossians 1:12)*

5. The Holy Spirit is the pledge of our inheritance.

> *When you believed, you were marked in him with a seal, the prom-*
> *ised Holy Spirit, who is a deposit guaranteeing our inheritance until*
> *the redemption of those who are God's possession—to the praise of his*
> *glory. (Ephesians 1:13b–14)*

When my husband and I bought our home, we had to make a down payment. The down payment was a pledge that proved our intent to purchase the property and ability to make payments. In the same way, the presence and power of the Holy Spirit in our lives is the pledge of our inheritance. The Spirit is demonstrable proof that God will give us everything He has promised.

When we talk about our inheritance in Christ, we emphasize God's gifts of grace. The blessings of salvation, our relationship with God, and life in God's kingdom are benefits we never could have achieved on our own. They are ours because God has adopted us as His children, purchasing us with the precious blood of Christ. "What was not ours by right has by God's grace now become our inalienable blessing."[4]

How should we respond to this glorious inheritance?

_____

_____

_____

_____

Our knowledge of our inheritance should stimulate our gratitude. Imagine that someone has given you a gift. Not just any gift—a gift perfectly chosen for you. A gift that takes into account all that you are. A gift greater than anything you would dream to ask for. A gift that was costly to the giver but given freely as an act of love. What do you say? *Thank you.* The words don't seem like enough, do they? Christ has given us something more precious than anything wrapped in paper and bows. He has given us Himself. Gratitude should be the natural outflow of our relationship with God.

How can you show gratitude for your inheritance in Christ?

_____

_____

_____

_____

Our knowledge of our inheritance should stimulate our confidence. "For God's gifts and his call are irrevocable" (Romans 11:29). God has given us our inheritance in Christ freely, and He will not take it away. No one can nullify or negate our status as children of God and joint heirs with Christ. We can live confidently that we are indeed God's children. If we doubt, the Holy Spirit's presence and power in our lives should reassure us that God will indeed keep His promises concerning us. We can live confidently because of the inheritance God graciously given us.

How does your understanding of your inheritance in Christ give you confidence in your relationship with Him?

_____

_____

Our knowledge of our inheritance should stimulate our hope. We have not yet received the fullness of our inheritance. Yet no matter how dark and grim this world may be, we know a better future awaits us in the kingdom of God—an inheritance that won't perish, spoil, or fade. Christ has guaranteed it for us by His own blood, and our hope in Him will never let us down.

How does the security of your inheritance in Christ give you hope?

_____

_____

_____

We've come a long way today! I hope you're beginning to glimpse the wonder and power of the inheritance Christ has given us. Like the daughters of Zelophehad, I pray that you step forward and embrace all that Christ wants to give you.

But there's one more aspect of inheritance we haven't covered today. Inheritances are meant to be stewarded. An inheritance isn't something we keep for ourselves. We also steward it so we can pass it on to the next generation. What implications does that have for our inheritance in Christ? Stick around. We'll start unpacking it tomorrow.

DAY FIVE

PASSING ON OUR INHERITANCE

We've talked about inheritance the last couple days, but there's one more quality of an inheritance we need to look at: Inheritances are meant to be passed on.

To examine what that means for us, we need to go back to the Daughters of Zelophehad again. When we left them in Numbers 27, it looked like everything was settled. Yet when Israel began dividing the land, a problem arose.

📖 Read Numbers 36:1–12 to see what happens.

What problem do the leaders of Manasseh bring to the Lord?

_____

_____

Why is that problem a concern for them?

_____

_____

What is the Lord's command regarding that problem?

_____

_____

As we've seen already this week, for Israel their inheritance of the land was a symbol not only of social belonging but of their relationship with the Lord. To be cut off from the land represented being cut off from the community and from God. For this reason, the ancestral inheritance could never be truly sold. All land was to revert to the ancestral families every fifty years during the year of Jubilee (Leviticus 25:13–17).

However, if Mahlah, Tirzah, Hoglah, Milkah, and Noah married outside their tribe, this created a problem. They would become members of their husband's clans, and their portions of land originally allotted to the tribe of Manasseh would become the property of another tribe Manasseh would lose a portion of their divine inheritance—something that was repugnant for faithful Israelites. When they brought the problem before the Lord, God commanded that the five sisters must keep their inheritance within the tribe by marrying members of the tribe of Manasseh.

For we modern women who are used to marrying whomever we please, this might seem like a harsh restriction. It probably felt like less of a burden for women living in a time when most marriages were arranged by their fathers or other male relatives. At any rate, the daughters of Zelophehad—who seem to have had no trouble speaking for themselves—didn't register any protest. They married cousins on their father's side, and their inheritance stayed within the family.

This episode reminds us of another important principle about inheritances, though: _Inheritances are meant to be passed on._

Inheritances are a gift we benefit from, but they are also a trust we steward. We are meant to use them, protect them, grow them and pass them on to the next generation. That's how we leave a legacy. Tangible or intangible, inheritances are something we are meant to pass on.

What inheritances have you received from family, friends, or mentors? Think both tangibly and intangibly.

_____

_____

_____

How are you stewarding those gifts?

_____

_____

How are you passing them on to others?

_____

_____

_____

Our divine inheritance is also meant to be passed on. Remember, the inheritance we receive from Christ was not ours by birth. God gave it to us when He adopted us as His children. By His grace He made us joint heirs with Christ and bestowed every blessing in the heavens on us. That blessing is not ours to hoard. Ours to treasure, yes. Ours to cherish. Ours to steward. It is also ours to pass on.

When we talk about inheritances of money, property, or land, the amount each person gets grows smaller the more it is divided. That's one reason family squabbles can get so bitter when it comes to dividing up the estate. When we start worrying about getting less because someone else gets more, it sets the stage for conflict.

God's economy doesn't work that way. We don't get smaller shares of God's kingdom because more people join the family. Grace multiplies, the kingdom grows, and we all get the full measure of God's blessing poured out on us. In Christ, we don't operate from a position of scarcity. We operate from a position of abundance. This frees us to live generously.

📖 Read 2 Corinthians 9:6–8 below. Underline the word "generously" as it occurs in these verses:

> Remember this: Whoever sows sparingly will also reap sparingly, and whoever sows generously will also reap generously. Each of you should give what you have decided in your heart to give, not reluctantly or under compulsion, for God loves a cheerful giver. And God is able to bless you abundantly, so that in all things at all times, having all that you need, you will abound in every good work.

How should we give and why should we give?

_____

_____

_____

What are the results of our generosity?

_____

_____

_____

📖 Read verse 8 again. What is God's promise to us?

_____

_____

_____

God's abundance toward us frees us to live generously toward others. We have the promise from God that when we live generously, He gives us what we need to participate in His kingdom work.

This attitude of abundance is not only meant for our material possessions. Our inheritance is God's gift of grace, and we are meant to pass it on by inviting others to accept God's gracious gift of salvation.

📖 Read 2 Corinthians 5:18–20.

What ministry do we have?

_____

_____

What is the message of this ministry?

_____

_____

_____

What does it mean to be ambassadors of reconciliation? Who do we represent? What message do we carry?

_____

_____

_____

We represent God to the world, pleading with those around us to be reconciled to God. This is what it means to steward and pass on the inheritance of God's grace. As though God were making the appeal through us, we implore others to come to Christ and be reconciled to God.

Maybe as you're reading this you have realized you have never been reconciled to God. You've never asked God to forgive your sins, never truly committed to following Christ as Lord. If that's true of you, I invite you now to turn to the appendix and read the steps and prayer written out there. It will walk you through how you can also be reconciled to God and receive the inheritance of grace God wants to give you.

But if you're reading this and like me, you have accepted God's amazing gift of grace, then we have a job to do. The gift God has given us is too priceless to keep to ourselves. We need to share it with others. And by the nature of God's divine economy, our inheritance doesn't shrink as others join the family. It grows. Sharing our inheritance of faith with others helps us leave a legacy.

How have people in your life passed on their inheritance of faith to you?

_____

_____

_____

_____

_____

How are you passing on your inheritance of faith to others?

_____

_____

_____

_____

As we close out this week, take a few moments to pray and thank God for the glorious inheritance of grace He has given us. Ask God to give you opportunities to share it with others. Write your prayer out below.

_____

_____

_____

_____

And be sure to stick around for next week. We'll be studying Abigail—a woman who left a legacy of wisdom and courage.

I can't wait for you to meet her.

LESSON 2

ABIGAIL
CALLING OTHERS INTO THEIR DESTINY

DAY ONE

MEET ABIGAIL

Abigail was a wise and beautiful woman who was married to a fool—quite literally. Abigail's husband's name, Nabal, is one of the Hebrew words for "fool." Nabal's foolishness set him on a collision course with David, Israel's future king. Abigail's well-timed words of wisdom turned David aside from his path of vengeance—a path that might well have prevented him from becoming king. Her story is primarily told in a single chapter of Scripture, but Abigail's courage and wisdom left a legacy of faith we can learn from.

Abigail's story is fit for the silver screen, but some background helps us grasp the drama and weight of her story. Abigail lived during the reign of Israel's first king, King Saul. Although Saul reigned over Israel, Saul's sin had led God to reject him as king. The Lord chose David to take his place. Saul did not take this news well. Driven by jealousy and fear, Saul vowed to destroy David. He set out on a vendetta, chasing David around the countryside as David and his men scrambled to stay out of Saul's reach. Though God had chosen David to succeed Saul as king, David refused to take matters into his own hands. David steadfastly chose to honor Saul as king and refused to lift his hand against Saul.

IN THEIR SHOES
Acts of Mercy

David twice had the opportunity to kill Saul, but both times David chose to spare Saul's life. David refused to lift his hand against the man God had anointed king. (1 Samuel 24:1–21; 26:1–25).

While David was on the run, he and his men camped for a time close to Nabal's home in Carmel. David and his men protected Nabal's shepherds as they cared for his flocks. His military band did not harass the shepherds or steal from them. Instead, they became a "wall" around them, making sure that the shepherds could discharge their duties in peace without being troubled by wild animals, bandits, or raiding parties from neighboring lands (1 Samuel 25:16).

When shearing time came around, David sent messengers to Nabal asking for a share of the bounty. It was customary for a landowner to reward his laborers at harvest time, and since David and his men had provided protection for Nabal, it was reasonable for them to expect some reward for their effort.

Nabal bluntly refused. In fact he did more than refuse—he insulted David and his men.

📖 Read 1 Samuel 25:10-11.

How did Nabal respond to David? Why might David have been insulted by his words?

Although Nabal claimed not to know who David was, it would have been virtually impossible for him not to be aware of David. His words indicate as much. Though David's men did not identify his heritage, Nabal recognized David as the "son of Jesse" (1 Samuel 25:10). This incident also happened after David had killed the giant Goliath, after he had served as Saul's military commander, and after Samuel had anointed David as king. How likely is it that a man as wealthy as Nabal would not have heard about this young warrior? Additionally, Nabal was from the same tribe as David. Nabal was a Calebite, and the Calebites were a clan from the tribe of Judah. Nabal must have surely known who David was, yet he intimated that David and his men were nothing more than a group of runaway slaves.

David's men went back and reported all that Nabal had said, and David told his men to strap on their swords.

Does this seem out of character for David, a man described elsewhere as a "man after God's own heart?"

Why do you think David might have been provoked to violence by Nabal's insult?

Sometimes even godly people are guilty of grievous sins. Anger, grief, and other strong emotions can cloud our decision making. What emotions can make you more prone to rash decisions?

How can we avoid falling into sin when our emotions are strong?

One of the servants went to Abigail and told her everything Nabal had said, reiterating how David and his men had protected them while they were in the fields. Scripture doesn't tell us where Abigail was when she heard the news. If I were filming it for the screen, I'd show her hard at work preparing food for the feast when she gets the word. Then I'd pan the camera to show her gaze as she looks at the crowd of people—children playing, women laughing as they set out food, men relaxing and celebrating with drink in hand—then cut back to a close-up of Abigail's face as she realizes that her husband's foolish words have put them all at risk. In a flash, Abigail recognizes what her husband had not. David would not take this insult lightly.

Abigail jumped into action. Without pausing to reason with Nabal, Abigail commanded the servants to prepare a large amount of food and load it on donkeys. She sent the servant and donkeys on ahead of her as she followed behind.

Again the scene is worthy of cinema. As Abigail rides her donkey into a mountain ravine, she looks up and sees David and his men coming toward her. Abigail slides off her donkey and bows down to David in a show of humility and respect. Then she delivers a prophetic speech that epitomizes diplomacy, tact, and wisdom.

📖 Read Abigail's words to David in 2 Samuel 25:23–31.

How would you describe Abigail's speech to David? How does she craft her message to appeal to him?

Has there ever been a time in your life when someone has pleaded with you to change your direction? What happened? How did you respond?

Abigail pleaded with David not to resort to unnecessary bloodshed and reminded him of the kind of king God had called him to be. David heeded her words, accepted the gift she had brought, and sent Abigail home in peace.

When Abigail returned home she found Nabal drunk and feasting like a king. She waited to tell Nabal what had happened until the next morning when he was sober. When he heard the news, Nabal "became like a stone" (1 Samuel 25:37.) We can't say for sure what happened, but it's possible he had a stroke or something similar.

Nabal died ten days later. When David heard the news, he recognized that God had avenged him and prevented him from doing wrong. God had brought Nabal's foolishness back upon him. David sent word to Abigail, asking her to become his wife. Abigail agreed. She gathered her servants and went to David. Abigail became David's wife.

Abigail's actions demonstrate wisdom and courage. She prevented David from turning insult into tragedy and reminded him what it meant to be God's anointed king. Like Abigail, we can find the courage to live wisely in a foolish world, to rise above our circumstances, and use our words to inspire others to be the people God has called them to be.

Speaking wisely? Living courageously? Inspiring others? That's what it looks like to leave a legacy.

DAY TWO

A WOMAN OF COURAGE AND WISDOM

First Samuel introduces Abigail as an "intelligent and beautiful woman" (25:3). Her actions demonstrate prudence, wisdom, and an understanding of how God was working in her world. Abigail both had the insight to understand God's will and the courage to carry it out.

The Hebrew word used to describe Abigail's wisdom is *sekel*. *Sekel* means *understanding, wisdom, prudence,* or *discretion.*

Read the following verses to get a better understanding of *sekel*:

The fear of the LORD is the beginning of wisdom [sekel]; all who follow his precepts have good understanding. (Psalm 111:10)

Prudence [sekel] is a fountain of life to the prudent, but folly brings punishment to fools. (Proverbs 16:22)

Good judgment [sekel] wins favor, but the way of the unfaithful leads to their destruction. (Proverbs 13:15)

How would you describe *sekel*? Write your definition in the space below.

How did Abigail's actions demonstrate this kind of prudent, practical wisdom?

Unlike her husband, Abigail had the foresight to recognize that Nabal's insults to David would bring destruction on her household. She quickly sprang into action to intervene, but her words to David also demonstrate that her actions flowed from her insight into what God was doing. Despite the risks, Abigail acted to protect her household and prevent David from instigating unnecessary violence.

Walter Bruggeman points out that the text introduces Nabal's possessions before it introduces him.[5] Nabal's wealth defines him. Throughout the passage Nabal's chief concerns are accumulating wealth, protecting his wealth, and indulging himself by enjoying his wealth.

With this in mind, read 1 Samuel 25:18. How would you describe the gift Abigail prepared for David? What risks might Abigail have been taking by preparing such an extravagant gift without telling her husband—especially after Nabal had refused to give David anything?

Abigail's actions were for the good of her household and in Nabal's best interests, but he could easily have seen her actions as insubordination. Abigail knew as she loaded her donkeys that she would have to tell her churlish, foolish husband what she had done. Though it was the right thing to do, she knew he would be displeased.

Abigail faced the risk of her husband's anger as she set out, but she also faced the risk of an angry warrior ahead of her.

Read 1 Samuel 25:21-22. How would you describe David's mood at this point in the story? What were David's intentions?

Abigail acted quickly to save her household, but she also intended to prevent David from an act of violence and revenge.

What do you think Abigail might have been thinking and feeling as she headed out to meet David? What risks was she taking by putting herself in the path of an angry warrior bent on revenge?

_____

_____

_____

Abigail's actions were risky, but she found the courage to do what is right. Abigail's actions are reminiscent of the poetic portrait of a wise woman in Proverbs 31.

📖 Read Proverbs 31:10–31. How does Abigail show the qualities of a wise woman as reflected in this passage?

_____

_____

_____

One of the interesting things about the portrait of a wise woman in Proverbs 31 is that the poem uses military language to describe this wise woman. Even the phrase translated "a wife of noble character" uses a phrase that the Old Testament often uses to describe warriors as "men of valor." Though the language is obscured somewhat in our English translations, other phrases in the poem also convey the image of battle. The Hebrew word translated "food" in verse 15 also means "prey." The phrase "lacks nothing of value" can also be translated "does not lack plunder." The first phrase of Verse 17, "She sets about her work vigorously," literally reads "she girds up her loins"—a common biblical image for preparing for battle or for difficult work.[6] The wise woman described in Proverbs 31 is a good wife, prudent household manager, and shrewd business woman, but she also has a warrior spirit.

Warrior may not be the first image we would associate with _wisdom_, but it makes sense when you stop to think about it. It takes courage and strength to live wisely in a foolish world.

Why do we need courage to live wisely? Where can we find that source of strength?

_____

_____

_____

📖 Read Proverbs 9:10 and write it out in the space below.

What is the beginning of wisdom?

Fearing the Lord doesn't mean the knees quaking, shoulders trembling kind of fear. The fear of the Lord is the deep respect and awe we feel in the Lord's presence. It reminds us that God is God, and we are not and that we must not take the Lord's holiness lightly. God demands our respect, our honor, and our undivided allegiance. When we know who God is and who we are in relationship to Him, we begin to find wisdom.

How can knowing God and living in relationship with Him give us the courage to live with wisdom?

In what areas of your life you need courage to live wisely?

How could your relationship with God give you the courage you need? Be specific. Finish the sentence. Because God is _____, I can _____.

DAY THREE

WHEN FAITHFULNESS AND FOOLISHNESS COLLIDE

Abigail was wise and courageous, but her husband was a fool. The Old Testament has five different words for "fool," each one with a slightly different nuance. Nabal's name is the Hebrew word for a recalcitrant, stubborn fool.

Read the following verses. What do they tell us about the character of a *nabal*?

The fool [nabal] says in his heart, "There is no God." (Psalm 14:1)

Remember how the enemy has mocked you, LORD, how foolish people [nabal] have reviled your name. (Psalm 74:18)

Eloquent lips are unsuited to a godless fool [nabal]—how much worse lying lips to a ruler!" (Proverbs 17:7)

For fools [nabal] speak folly, their hearts are bent on evil: They practice ungodliness and spread error concerning the LORD. (Isaiah 32:6)

Based on these verses, how would you describe a *nabal*?

_____

_____

📖 As described in 1 Samuel 25, how does Nabal's character reflect his name?

_____

_____

What do you think life was like for Abigail to be married to a man like Nabal?

_____

_____

I can't imagine that Abigail's life with Nabal was anything close to ideal. Nabal was a prominent and wealthy man, but he was also the kind of fool who denies the existence of God and whose heart is bent on evil. He was surly and mean (1 Samuel 25:3) and arrogant enough that he denied David food, then feasted like a king while God's annointed king and his men were going hungry. While Abigail was remarkably in touch with what God was doing, Nabal was blind to anything but his own pleasure.

Yet Abigail chose to be faithful. It might have been easy for Abigail to do nothing—to stay in her place and let Nabal's foolishness come down on his own head. Instead, Abigail chose to take initiative and do what was right. Though her circumstances were not ideal, Abigail was faithful to God and who God had called her to be.

Maybe like Abigail, you're serving in a place where your circumstances aren't ideal. Perhaps there's a Nabal in your life—a spouse, an employer, a teacher, or another authority figure whose lack of morals and foolish behavior make life miserable for you. Or perhaps your circumstances are difficult in other ways. You struggle with a difficult marriage or with a child who combats you at every turn. You're a caregiver for someone who can't or won't appreciate the depth of your sacrifice, or you're dealing with your own set of stresses surrounding finances, chronic illness, or other pressures. Whatever your circumstances, you find yourself thinking that one day things will get better. *One day when things are easier I can serve God. One day . . .*

Abigail reminds us that there is never a perfect time. All we have are the moments we are given—not some Instagram-worthy snapshot of what we wish our reality was like. Our choice is not whether or not we will be faithful in some perfect future, but whether we will be faithful *today*, no matter the circumstances we are in.

First Peter was written to a group of believers who, like Abigail, were living in a situation that was less than ideal. The churches of Asia Minor were experiencing persecution. They had become the targets of slander and social ostracism and were experiencing economic pressures. Some were slaves serving pagan masters, and some were Christian women married to unbelieving men. Both groups grappled with how to be faithful to God while living under the authority of people who did not know the Lord.

📖 Read 1 Peter 2:11–17.

What does this passage say about how we should live faithfully in circumstances that are not ideal?

_____

_____

_____

What are the results when we live faithfully in difficult circumstances?

_____

_____

What attitude should we show to people who live foolishly and who treat us poorly?

_____

_____

I want to add an important caveat here: neither this passage nor Abigail's story are talking about what we should do in cases of abuse. Nowhere in Scripture does it say that you should stay and submit to an abusive situation. If someone in your life is subjecting you to physical, emotional, spiritual, or sexual abuse, your priority needs to be getting yourself safe. If you need help, you'll find the contact information for the National Domestic Abuse Hotline in the back of the book. They can help you make a plan to get safe.

For many of us, though, we are not dealing with abusive and potentially dangerous situations. What we are grappling with are situations that are difficult and unfair, relationships that are challenging, and circumstances that press us to the point that we're not sure we can go on. When we face those circumstances, how can we live faithfully?

First, we need to be proactive and courageous about doing good. When our circumstances are not ideal, it is easy to draw inside ourselves and not look outside the circle of our own pain. Yet God always gives us opportunities to bless others. When we are attentive to the people God places in our path, we can be channels of God's love and grace. It may be as simple as a kind word or a smile, but by resolutely doing good we bring glory to God and reveal the foolish insults and empty accusations of others for what they are.

We also need to yield to the authorities God has placed over us. Again, this does not mean putting ourselves in vulnerable positions. It also does not mean going along with actions or commands we know to be wrong. Perhaps you have a boss who is unfair and seems to be out to get you. Yielding to his authority means being on time to work, doing your job to the best of your ability, and being polite and respectful in your interactions with him. It may also mean using the appropriate resources of your company policy and the human resources department to protect yourself and other vulnerable people at your company. It does not give you permission to be passive-aggressive, disrespectful of his position, or work to undermine him behind his back. His lack of integrity does not invalidate yours.

People in authority over us may be ungodly, foolish, and corrupt. The Roman government was no bastion of morality, but Peter still urged Christians to submit to governmental authority. By living according to the laws of their society, Christians revealed themselves to be decent, good people and silenced the ignorant talk of people who accused them of sedition and disrespect. We can do the same.

Finally, living faithfully in less than ideal circumstances means remembering whom we serve. Ultimately, we are servants of God. We see this in Abigail's life. Although Nabal was her husband, she was accountable to a higher authority. She took steps to make sure that her actions were pleasing to God. We have freedom as children of God, but we should not use that freedom as an excuse to do evil. We are accountable to God, and we must do what is pleasing in His sight.

Have you ever been challenged to live faithfully in circumstances that were less than ideal? What did you do?

How could Abigail's story encourage you to be faithful the next time you face difficult circumstances?

DAY FOUR

CHOOSING OUR WORDS WELL

One of the things that makes Abigail stand out is her courageous speech to David. Abigail's words are a model of wisdom, diplomacy, and respect.

📖 Read 1 Samuel 25:23-31.

How does Abigail craft her speech to appeal to David?

What is the goal of Abigail's speech?

How does she speak truth to David?

How would you describe Abigail's attitude as she speaks to David?

Abigail models for us how to use our words well. To leave a legacy of faith, we must learn how to harness the power of our words.

Think of a person of influence in your life. How did that person encourage you with their words?

Words can encourage, but words can also wound. How has someone used their words to hurt you? What effect did those words have on you?

As a child, my mother took me to have my picture taken one afternoon. I had on a navy dress with white polka dots, and I obediently posed for pictures. The photographer kept coaxing me to smile bigger, and I finally smiled wide enough to show my crooked teeth. The photographer turned to my mother and said, "She hides those good, doesn't she?" Looking back as an adult, I don't know that the photographer meant anything negative by it. But in the moment, what I heard was "There's something wrong with her smile." Even after I got braces, it took me years to teach myself to smile for photos and show my teeth again.

Words have power to wound or to heal. We can use our words to destroy reputations, turn people against one another, or cut people down with our anger and bitterness. We can also use our words to build one another up, to point people to Christ, to gently deliver correction where it is needed, and to call people to be their best versions of themselves.

Read the following verses about how we should use our speech:

"Do not let any unwholesome talk come out of your mouths, but only what is helpful for building others up according to their needs, that it may benefit those who listen." (Ephesians 4:29)

"Therefore each of you must put off falsehood and speak truthfully to your neighbor, for we are all members of one body." (Ephesians 4:25)

"But now you must also rid yourselves of all such things as these: anger, rage, malice, slander, and filthy language from your lips. Do not lie to each other, since you have taken off your old self with its practices and have put on the new self, which is being renewed in knowledge of the image of its Creator." (Colossians 3:8-10)

"Let the message of Christ dwell among you richly as you teach and admonish one another with all wisdom through psalms, hymns, and songs from the Spirit, singing to God with gratitude in your hearts. And whatever you do, whether in word or deed, do it all in the name of the Lord Jesus, giving thanks to God the Father through him." (Colossians 3:16-17)

What do these verses say about how we should not use our speech?

_____

_____

What do these verses say about how we should use our speech?

_____

_____

How do Abigail's words to David line up with the truth of these verses?

_____

_____

Because our words have such power, we should use our speech to bring glory to God. Yet this is challenging for all of us.

My biggest challenge in my speech is not so much saying the wrong thing as it is not saying the right thing. I'm a bottler. I can chat just fine in small groups, but in large groups of people I'm content to sit and listen. If I have to talk over other people or fight to be heard, I tend to stay silent. I'm also an internal processor. I like to have time to reflect and plan out what I'm going to say rather than just speaking off the cuff. Those aren't bad qualities, but it does mean that it's easy for me to stay silent rather than speaking a truth that needs to be heard. It can also mean that my silence can be misread as agreement when I'm actually trying to avoid an argument or can't get a word in edgewise. For me, using my words well can mean stepping out of my comfort zone and opening my mouth to speak truth and build others up.

I have a sweet friend who's at the other end of the spectrum: a blurter. She's the life of the party and never meets a stranger. She's an external processor, so she tends to think out loud, blurting out her thoughts as they cross her mind. That's not a bad thing. Her vividness and willing to speak uncomfortable truths are powerful. However, sometimes she leaves hurt feelings in her wake because she's so busy talking that she doesn't fine tune her speech or recognize how her words are affecting others. For her, using her speech well can mean pausing to make sure she is speaking what is needful in the moment and glorifying God with the words that come out of her mouth.

What challenges might bottlers have in using their words well? How can they glorify God with their words?

What challenges might blurters have in using their words well? How can blurters glorify God with their words?

Are you more of a bottler or a blurter? How can Abigail's example motivate you to use your words well?

CALLING OTHERS INTO THEIR DESTINIES

One of the most powerful ways we can use our words is to call other people into their destinies. Sometimes we all need those reminders to live like who we are meant to be. As Abigail reminded David of the kind of king God intended him to be, we can challenge others—and ourselves—to be the people God has created us to be.

David was a man after God's own heart, but he was not a perfect person. However, David showed great restraint in his interactions with Saul. Saul was in many ways an utter failure as king, but David would not take matters into his own hands. He was content to wait until God delivered the kingdom to him, and he did not rush matters by seeking vengeance.

David's interactions with Saul show that he was capable of great patience and discretion. Yet in his interaction with Nabal, David let Nabal's foolishness provoke him to anger. David was so furious that he was willing to take out his anger on Nabal and his entire household, perhaps even slaughtering some of the same shepherds David and his men had protected in the wilderness.

God had chosen David to replace Saul as king. When God sent the prophet Samuel to find the young David and anoint him as king, David was out in the fields caring for his father's sheep. As a shepherd, part of David's duties were to provide for the needs of the sheep and protect them from predators such as lions and bears. It was an apt metaphor for the kind of king God intended David to be. God wanted David to shepherd His people, finally uniting the loose connection of tribes into a strong nation and renewing their worship of the Lord. God also intended for David to defend Israel, protecting the people from the surrounding nations that might attack them in the same way he had protected his sheep from the lions and bears that went after the flock. If David had followed through on his intentions to slaughter Nabal and his men, David would have violated his role as shepherd and protector of the people.

📖 Read 1 Samuel 25:23-35. What warning does Abigail give David?

_____

_____

How does Abigail remind David of his destiny?

_____

_____

How does David respond to Abigail's warning?

_____

_____

God placed Abigail in David's path to turn him away from an act of violence and bloodshed. Abigail saved the lives of the men of her household, but she also prevented David from committing an act that could have jeopardized his destiny. David could not rule over Israel if he spilled innocent blood.

Sometimes in life we may be like David. We need people in our lives who are willing to speak truth to us, turning us aside from paths that are contrary to God's best for our lives. We need to be teachable, willing to listen and consider it when people who desire God's best for us confront us with what may be uncomfortable truths.

Has anyone ever been like Abigail to you, speaking words to you that convicted you of sin or caused you to reconsider a decision you had made? How did you respond?

Sometimes in life we may also be like Abigail. We need to courageously and faithfully go to people in our lives, reminding them of who God has called them to be. When we do this, our goal is not to tear down or destroy. Our goal is to reconcile and redeem, pointing people back to God and His plan for their lives.

Have you ever been like Abigail to someone? What did you do? How did the other person respond?

To call people into their destinies, we must learn to see them as God sees them. Though our social media-driven culture makes it easy to connect with people around the world, our addiction to our phones can make it easy for us to treat people as disposable. It only takes a click to block, hide, or unfriend. When we are in real relationships with real people, we cannot and should not shove them aside at the first hint of frailty, conflict, or mistakes. The people around us are made in the image of God and intended for Christ's glory. We must learn to look for the new creation God is making them to be.

📖 Read 2 Corinthians 5:16–17.

What does it mean to regard someone from a worldly point of view?

How can seeing people as new creations in Christ change our viewpoint of them?

How might this new perspective help us call people into their destiny?

It takes wisdom and insight to see the potential in others. Yet when we are willing to take the time to see as Christ sees them, we can become women who encourage others to be the people God has made them to be. We can be women who with a well-timed word encourage people to turn from sin, embrace Christ, and discover the calling God has placed on their lives.

You have a calling on your life. So do the people God has placed around you. Helping others discover and live out their God-ordained destinies is one way we can leave legacies.

LESSON 3

HULDAH
COMMITTED TO GOD'S WORD

DAY ONE

A WOMAN COMMITTED TO GOD'S WORD

We know few of the details of Huldah's story, but what we do know has significance. Huldah was a prophet—one of three female prophets named in the Old Testament. She was dedicated to the Word of God, and she had the ear of the king.

That's all she needed to usher in revival.

To understand Huldah's story, it's helpful for us to understand the times in which she lived. For us to do that, we need to back up and do a little Old Testament history.

During his reign, David united the nation of Israel around the worship of the Lord. His son, Solomon, built the temple and also reigned over a united Israel, but Solomon's taxes and use of conscripted labor caused resentment among some of the northern tribes. When Solomon's son, Rehoboam, said he would intensify his father's policies, the ten northern tribes broke away from the house of David. David's descendants continued to reign over the southern nation of Judah, and a new king rose to rule over the northern kingdom of Israel.

 **DID YOU KNOW?**
Jeroboam

Jeroboam was the first king to lead Israel after it split from Judah. His first act as king was to erect two golden calves for the people to worship. The northern kingdom never had another king who led them back to whole-hearted devotion to God.

Both Israel and Judah began a downward spiral in their relationship with the Lord. During the time of the divided kingdom, Israel never had a king who followed the Lord. The northern kingdom went into Assyrian exile in 722 BC, leaving Judah alone in a sea of international powers. Like the kings of Israel, many of the kings of Judah also turned away from the Lord, but there were bright spots. One of those was King Hezekiah, who led the people in a great revival. Even as Assyria carried Israel into exile, Hezekiah saw the Lord miraculously deliver Judah from destruction.

Hezekiah was faithful to God. His son, King Manasseh, was not. Manasseh ruled over Israel for fifty-five years, and "he did evil in the sight of the LORD" (2 Kings 21:2). Hezekiah had destroyed many of the altars and high places on Israel's hills where people worshiped idols, but Manasseh rebuilt them. Manasseh went so far as to place pagan altars in the temple of the Lord. He burned his own son as a pagan sacrifice, and "shed so much innocent blood that he filled Jerusalem from end to end" (2 Kings 21:16). God vowed to punish Judah because of Manasseh's sin.

📖 Read 2 Kings 21:1-5. What do you think it would have been like to live as a faithful Jew during the time of Manasseh? What challenges might people have faced who were faithful to the Lord?

_____

_____

_____

After Manasseh died, his son Amon became king. Amon followed in his father's footsteps. He only ruled over Israel for two years before some of his court officials staged a coup and assassinated the king in his own palace. Amon's son Josiah became king in his place. Josiah was only eight years old.

Instead of following in the footsteps of his father and grandfather, Josiah chose a different path. Josiah followed the Lord. In the eighth year of his reign, when Josiah was sixteen years old, he began to seek the Lord (2 Chronicles 34:3). He tore down the pagan altars and purged the land of the pagan priests. In the eighteenth year of his reign, Josiah turned his attention to the temple. The temple had not been renovated since before Manasseh's reign—well over sixty years ago. Josiah commanded his secretary to work with the high priest in funding and completing renovations on the temple. In the process of restoring the temple, High Priest Hilkiah made a remarkable discovery:

📖 Read 2 Kings 22:8-10. What does Hilkiah find? What surprises you about this discovery?

_____

_____

_____

We live in a world where nine out of ten American homes has a Bible, and the average household has three.[7] With Scripture so easily available on our bookshelves and smartphones, it might be hard for us to understand how something as important as the Book of the Law could actually be lost and forgotten. It helps to remember that the world of ancient Israel was very different than ours. In a primarily oral society like Israel, few people could read and write. Written records were expensive to produce, meaning there were probably not many copies of Scripture to begin with. As Manasseh placed pagan altars within the temple courts and "filled Jerusalem with innocent blood," we can only imagine that the priests who valued these scrolls lost influence and access to the temple. In ancient times, people often stored valuable objects in walls or foundations. Perhaps someone had tucked the precious scroll into a wall of the temple for safekeeping, not knowing it would be forgotten for sixty years. However it happened, Hilkiah found the book during the process of renovation and brought it straight to the king.

📖 Read 2 Kings 22:11–13.

How does King Josiah respond to hearing what God had said in the book of the law?

We don't know exactly what portion of the Law Hilkiah found, but based on Josiah's reaction and subsequent reforms, most scholars believe it was a portion of the book of Deuteronomy. Deuteronomy summarizes Israel's covenant responsibilities to God. It also explains the blessings of living in covenant with God and the consequences of breaking covenant. When Josiah heard God's Word read for the first time, he was deeply grieved. He needed to know if these words were truly the words of God. He sent several of his court officials to find out. They went straight to Huldah.

📖 Read 2 Kings 22:14–20.

Put Huldah's answer in your own words. What is her message to the king?

What stands out to you about Huldah's message?

What do Huldah's words tell us about her? About her relationship with God?

Huldah confirmed that the book of the law Hilkiah had found was God's Word and that all God had said in it was true. Yet she also left Josiah with hope. Because Josiah had repented, God would delay His judgment. The court officials took Huldah's message back to the king, and Josiah responded by calling the people together for a public act of repentance and renewal of the covenant. Huldah's commitment to Scripture prompted Josiah to usher in revival.

Isn't this a fascinating story? We've painted the broad strokes, and now we'll start digging into the details. Tomorrow we'll take a look at Huldah's dedication to God's Word—and what it looks like for us to share her commitment.

Day Two

A Track Record of Faithfulness

As I read this story, there's one question I keep asking myself: Why Huldah? It's a logical question. As king, Josiah had his pick of prophets. Jeremiah was already active by this time in Josiah's reign (Jeremiah 1:2). Zephaniah also prophesied during Josiah's reign. Like Josiah, Zephaniah was a grandson of King Hezekiah, making him a relative of the young king.

So why did Josiah's men go to Huldah—a woman completely unknown outside of this one account in Scripture? Part of it may have been proximity. As a resident of Jerusalem's New Quarter, it was easy for the king's men to find Huldah. Part of it may also have been age. Jeremiah was young when he began prophesying, and his youth and relative lack of experience may have meant that the king's men ruled him out. Similarly, as a grandson of Hezekiah, Zephaniah was likely a contemporary of Josiah's. If Huldah was an older woman, the king's advisors may have sought her out as a voice of wisdom and experience.

I think it is likely that Huldah brought life experience along with her prophetic gift. I suspect, however, that there was another reason the king's men went to Huldah. Confronted with this previously lost portion of Scripture, Josiah had a specific question: Were the words on this scroll the words of God? And if so, what would happen to Josiah and the nation of Judah for their failure to keep their covenant with God. The king didn't just need a prophet; he needed a prophet who was dedicated to God's word. Is it possible that the king's men went to Huldah because she had a reputation for being committed to the word of God?

I believe this is what set Huldah apart: she had an unflinching commitment to God's word. Her message to Josiah was not a pleasant one to deliver. Judgment was coming. Yet she emphasized that the scroll Josiah had heard read was indeed the Word of God. God would do everything written in the scroll, just as He had said.

But what was in this scroll? Why did Josiah react to it so strongly? Again, we don't know for certain, but since Josiah's reforms seem to be based on the Book of Deuteronomy, it seems likely that the scroll in question was a portion of Deuteronomy.

Deuteronomy 28 summarizes the blessings and curses of Israel's covenant with God.

📖 Read Deuteronomy 28.

What are some of Israel's responsibilities under the covenant?

How would God bless Israel if they kept their covenant with the Lord?

What are some of the consequences Israel would face if they broke their covenant with God?

Under Mannessah's reign, has Israel kept or broken their covenant with God? How?

What were some of the potential consequences Israel faced for breaking their covenant with God?

We can't say for certain what portion of the law Josiah heard, but from his reaction it seems to have been a passage much like Deuteronomy 28—a passage that clearly outlined Israel's responsibility to God and the consequences they faced of breaking covenant with God. Josiah knew Israel had failed God and had begun to set things right, but it seems he had not comprehended how deep Israel's failure went or how severe the consequences of that failure might be. Hearing the words of the Lord read for the first time devastated the young king, and he mourned.

Faced with the king's men, Huldah had a choice. Would she verify the difficult truth of the scroll, or would she offer false comfort?

📖 Read 2 Kings 22:15–20.

How do Huldah's words compare to what we read in Deuteronomy 28?

_____

_____

_____

How easy do you think it would have been for Huldah to deliver this message to the king?

_____

_____

_____

Huldah challenges me to remember that being committed to Scripture requires me to be committed to all of Scripture.

Let's be honest: there are often parts of the Bible we like more than others. It's easy for us to read beautiful poetry like Psalm 23 or lyrical passages about love like 1 Corinthians 13. We like passages that are encouraging and make us feel good, but passages that convict us and warn us about the consequences of sin are harder to cope with. Yet all Scripture is written by God. We cannot pick and choose the parts we like. We must embrace all the truth God has given us.

📖 Read 1 Timothy 2:16–17 below:

> _All Scripture is God-breathed and is useful for teaching, rebuking,_
> _correcting, and training in righteousness, so that the servant of God_
> _may be thoroughly equipped for every good work._

Underline the word _all_ at the beginning of the verse. How much of Scripture is God-breathed—God inspired?

_____

This passage gives us four ways Scripture is useful for us. List them below:

1. _____

2. _____

3. _____

4. _____

Circle the words _so that_ in the verse. _So that_ is usually an indicator of purpose—the reason why something is provided. According to this verse, what is the purpose of Scripture?

_____

God gives us Scripture to equip us through teaching us, rebuking us, correcting us, and training us in righteousness.

Is it comfortable to be taught, rebuked, corrected, and trained?

What would be the result if we only read the portions of Scripture that make us comfortable?

Scripture comforts us. It consoles and encourages us. Yet we must also allow Scripture to convict us.

Today, many people view portions of Scripture as optional. They argue about which of the letters Paul wrote, regard the New Testament as vital and the Old Testament as nonessential, or consider Jesus's words more authoritative than Paul's letters. Yet God tells us that all Scripture is God-breathed. There are passages that are difficult to understand and parts of Scripture we must wrestle with. Even so, our goal in reading the Bible is not to conform Scripture to us but to submit ourselves to it. To be committed to the Word, we must be committed to *all* of the Word—even the parts that challenge and convict.

How have you been convicted by Scripture?

What should our response be when we are convicted by Scripture?

Huldah reminds us of the importance of embracing the whole counsel of the Word of God. When Scripture challenges or convicts, don't fear wrestling with the hard truths. Aligning ourselves with the fullness of God's Word positions us to receive the fullness of God's blessing.

THE POWER OF THE WORD

One of my favorite pieces of kitchen equipment is our toaster oven and its power to turn ordinary pieces of bread into golden pieces of crispy toast. One morning I popped my piece of bread into the oven, punched the toast button, and went about fixing my breakfast. A few minutes later I came back to check on it, only to find my piece of bread sitting forlornly on the wire rack. The oven was dark and cold. I punched the button again. Nothing happened. The oven was several years old, and we decided it had gone out. Later that day my husband brought home a new toaster oven with all the bells and whistles. I eagerly unwrapped it and plugged it in, then punched the toast button. Again, nothing happened. The machine sat silently on the counter.. I had started to think we had bought a lemon when my husband went out to check the breaker. Suddenly the oven started working. It turned out the breaker switch had been thrown. The problem wasn't with my new toaster oven—or my old one. The problem was that there was no power going to the outlet.

Kitchen appliances need electricity to function. In the same way, we need God's power for our life and ministry.

📖 Read John 15:5 and write it out below:

_____

_____

_____

Underline the word *nothing* in the verse above. Jesus said that apart from Him we can do *nothing*. At times I've struggled with the reality of this verse. I like to see myself as a confident, capable, get-it-done type of person. If I don't know how to do something, there's always a book or a YouTube video that will show me how. And yet, the reality is that without Christ's power at work in me, I am incapable of doing anything of eternal significance. Staying connected to Jesus is the only way I can leave a legacy.

The same was true of Huldah. Huldah's message wasn't powerful because she was influential, charismatic, or capable. Huldah's message was powerful because God's Word is powerful.

📖 Read once more Huldah's words to the king from 2 Kings 22:15–20. What is the first thing Huldah said to the king?

_____

_____

The first words out of Huldah's mouth: "This is what the LORD, the God of Israel says." Huldah didn't go on a rant or give Josiah the piece of her mind she had been saving up.

She didn't worry about her brand or strike an Instagram-worthy pose. Huldah simply said what God wanted her to say. That's what gave her message its power.

Huldah's dedication to God's Word echoed something the apostle Paul would say some seven hundred years later in his first letter to the Corinthians:

> *When I came to you, I did not come with eloquence or human wisdom as I proclaimed to you the testimony about God. For I resolved to know nothing while I was with you except Jesus Christ and him crucified. I came to you in weakness with great fear and trembling. My message and my preaching were not with wise and persuasive words, but with a demonstration of the Spirit's power, so that your faith might not rest on human wisdom, but on God's power.*
> *(1 Corinthians 2:1–4)*

What is the core of Paul's preaching?

_____

_____

Why did Paul devote himself singly to the gospel and the Spirit's power?

_____

_____

Paul wanted the Corinthians faith to rest on Christ, not charisma. He knew that there were eloquent philosophers and religious teachers who tried to persuade their audiences with their wit and rhetorical skills. He set himself apart from them by preaching the unadorned gospel of Christ. All he needed to know or to preach was Jesus.

In the same way, Huldah knew that Josiah didn't need to hear from her. Josiah needed to hear from God. Huldah simply proclaimed the message the Lord had given her.

We live in a noisy world. Even as I'm writing this, I have to keep my internet off and my cell phone out of view to help myself shut out distractions. The constant lure of the world's noise is always there. How many likes or clicks do I have? How many followers? What do my metrics tell me about website clicks and subscriptions? What happens if I tweak this set of keywords or hashtags? What am I missing on the news, on the web, and on social media? And in all of that noise, what do I need to do to get my message heard?

But here's the thing. It's not my message that matters. It's God's. I can work on branding, practice speaking skills, and build a social media following. Yet without the foundation of God's word, all I can proclaim are cotton candy promises: words that sound pretty but only offer the illusion of substance. Have you ever seen what happens to cotton candy when it sits out too long? Those clouds of pink sugar fluff melt, leaving a sticky mess behind. If we want to leave a legacy, we must offer people more than cotton candy spirituality. We need to proclaim a message that matters: the meat and bread of God's Word.

Not all of us are ministers, speakers, authors, or social media mavens. But all of us have a story to tell: the glorious story of salvation God has entrusted to us. As we close out today, prayerfully reflect on the message God has entrusted to you. What is the word that God wants you to proclaim? What does it mean for you to know only Jesus Christ and Him crucified? And who needs to hear this powerful message God has given to you? Reflect on these questions in prayer and then journal about them in the space below.

Take time to thank God for the message He has given you and ask Him for the opportunity to proclaim it. When we speak God's unvarnished truth, we leave a legacy.

DAY FOUR

SPEAKING TRUTH TO POWER

It is difficult to speak truth to power. In his book, *Tempting Faith*, John Kuo shared his observations about the silent power of the Oval Office:

> Every president tells a similar story. They say they love sitting behind their desk knowing that the very important person they are about to see really wants to rip their head off about something or another, and knowing that the moment the person walks into the Oval Office he or she will cower at the weight of history and the weight of the presidency and say very little.[8]

We feel it in our own lives. Whether we are talking to an employer, a police officer, a principal, a spiritual leader, or a president, it is difficult to look powerful people in the eye and tell them that they are wrong.

Yet this is what Huldah had to do. It would have been easy for Huldah to sweep the message of the rediscovered book aside:

Oh, that was written in another time.

We've learned so much since then!

What God really meant to say was . . .

But God didn't mean you!

Prophets are not charged with speaking partial truths. God designates men and women as prophets who are willing to speak the hard truths, imagine the alternate reality God has designed for His people, and invite others to join us in living differently than the dominant culture. This was Huldah's task—to proclaim God's truth and encourage Josiah to persist in showing the people of Judah that there was another way to live. They didn't have to fall sway to the powerless idols their fathers had worshiped. They didn't have to be governed by fear. They could follow the harder and brighter path of returning to the Lord in repentance and embracing the fullness of God's will for them.

📖 Read again Huldah's message to Josiah in 2 Kings 22:15–20. Summarize her message in your own words.

What parts of Huldah's message might have been hard for her to deliver?

Imagine yourself in Huldah's shoes. How might you have felt giving a message like this to the king?

Where do you think Huldah found the courage to send this message back to King Josiah? Where did her confidence come from?

We may find ourselves asking difficult questions when it comes time to proclaim truth. For one thing, how do we know those who claim to speak truth really are truthful? And when it is our turn to speak truth, how do we know what and when we are to speak? Both of these questions can be answered by examining our message and our motivation.

Here's a simple question to ask when examining someones's message: *Is the message true to God's Word?* We've already seen that Huldah cleaved to the truth of God's Word and did not depart from it. All those who speak in the name of God must do the same.

📖 Read Hebrews 4:12. What is the Word of God able to do?

The Word of God is a sharp sword, able to divide even between soul and spirit. I've met many people who think they have insight into people's thoughts and motivation, and sometimes the Spirit of God does give us understanding of what lies beneath people's behaviors. Yet I've also observed that many people who think they have this kind of discernment are also prone to assigning their own personal motivations to other people and making assumptions about them based on their own presuppositions. The truth is that none of us are mind readers. Only the Spirit of God knows what lies within the human heart, and only the Word of God is the standard by which our thoughts and attitudes can be judged. Our job is not to judge others' inner lives but to proclaim truth. The Spirit is the one who convicts—not us.

But how do we know if others are proclaiming truth accurately? After all, even Satan quotes Scripture when it suits him. Here are some questions that can help:

Does this message align with the content of God's Word? Does it say what Scripture says? Are verses cherry picked or taken out of context? Are words twisted in meaning or "hidden" ideas revealed that make a passage say the opposite of its clear and direct meaning?

Does this message align with the purpose of God's Word? God always speaks with a redemptive purpose. Even in times of judgment, God also proclaims the hope to be found in repentance and salvation. His goal is conviction, not condemnation; restoration, not our destruction. Truth and grace are inseparable.

Does this message resonate with what the Spirit of God has already spoken to us? Does God speak through other believers? Absolutely. Yet most often I find that when God speaks to me through a member of my faith community, their voice resonates with or confirms what God has already spoken to me through His Word and His Spirit. If we want to hear God's voice, we don't have to look for a prophet, pastor, or popular figure to proclaim it to us. What we need is to seek God in prayer and in the Word, trusting that He will reveal Himself to us. If we are faithfully seeking God, we must use caution when someone claims to have a message for us God has not already spoken.

Discernment can help us sort through the messages others speak to us, but we must also use discernment when it comes time to speak truth to others. Like Huldah, we may be in the position of having to declare uncomfortable truths. But how do we know when we are following the prompting of God and when we are following our own desires or emotions? Even a message that is true to Scripture may do damage when spoken with the wrong motivation. Again, some basic questions can help us discern our motivations:

Is my desire to speak coming from a place of anger, pain, fear, or guilt? While the presence of these emotions does not mean we should not speak, it does mean that we need to use caution lest they mislead us.

Is my goal to destroy or to restore and protect? Our desire to speak should not be motivated by revenge or a desire to tear someone else down. Our purposes should be aligned with God's redemptive purpose.

Do I have the right to speak into this person's life? Huldah was able to speak to Josiah because the king invited her input. Truth is grounded best in relationship and community. Before I speak hard truths to someone, I need to consider if I have earned the right to do so either by relationship or invitation.

Do I have something to gain from this message? Huldah had nothing to gain and everything to lose by proclaiming her message to the king. If I have something to gain financially, socially, or emotionally by speaking this truth, I need to hit the pause button and cover it in prayer as I sort out my motivations.

Has God confirmed the necessity of this message to me over time? Before I confront someone with hard truths, I need to take time to be sure I am acting on what God has said and not the whims of the moment. We should not say it if we haven't taken time to pray it.

📖 King Josiah accepted Huldah's message. Read 2 Kings 23:1–25 to find out what happened.

What details of King Josiah's response stand out to you? Write a brief summary of the passage in the space provided below:

One of the reasons this passage intrigues me is that one of the king's roles was to lead the people in worship and honoring their covenant with God. Israel saw the land as belonging to God and understood that the Lord was Israel's true king. The kings of Israel and Judah served as understewards who had authority delegated to them by God. One of the king's chief responsibilities was to know the Law so that he could promote and fulfill it.

📖 Deuteronomy 17:18–20 describes the king's responsibility to know and follow the law. Read these verses in your Bible. What was the king supposed to do regarding the law? Why was it important?

According to Deuteronomy, the king of Israel was to take the priest's copy of the law and write out his own copy so that he could read it daily. He was to read it "all the days of his life so that he might learn to revere the Lord his God," "follow carefully" the fullness of the law, "not consider himself better than his fellow Israelites," and not "turn from it to the right or to the left." This daily dwelling on the Law would produce both obedience and humility. Yet because the Law had become lost, Josiah did not read the law in its fullness until the eighteenth year of his reign. Josiah's heart wasn't in the wrong place—he was simply ignorant of all that the law demanded.

How does this story speak to you about the importance of knowing the fullness of God's Word?

_____

_____

_____

We have a privilege Josiah did not have: the full and complete canon of God's Word.

Though we have the great blessing and privilege of stewarding promoting and upholding the Word of God, it is too easy to let our Bibles gather dust on our nightstands. We may not lose our copies of Scripture, but we can easily neglect them. Are there portions of Scripture you have not read? Parts that you are not as familiar with as you could be? If so, consider making a plan to read the Bible through in its entirety. Write your plan out below:

_____

_____

_____

_____

_____

_____

DAY FIVE

RENEWING THE COVENANT

After Huldah confirmed the authenticity of the scroll to Josiah, the king led the people in a covenant renewal ceremony. He led the people to come together and hear the Word of God, then led by example by personally renewing his covenant to God. Finally, the king led the people to renew their covenant with God. The covenant was a solemn binding agreement between their people and God in which the people vowed to serve the Lord with an undivided allegiance and to fully obey His word.

In what way do we as followers of Christ make covenant with God?

Has God ever led you to renew your commitment to your relationship with Him?

Josiah also purged the land of idols. It's interesting to me that although the king had begun repairing the temple, he did not remove the items of pagan worship from the temple until after he had found the scroll of the law and Huldah had confirmed its authenticity (2 Kings 23:4). Is it possible that idolatry had become so normalized in Israelite culture that even a king fully devoted to God didn't recognize idolatry for the sin that it was?

The tendency to normalize our idols is one of the things that makes idolatry so dangerous—and that is not a tendency unique to ancient Israel. Even in the New Testament we sometimes see that otherwise faithful believers accepted false teaching or compromised themselves by worshiping idols. If we fail to root our perspective deep in Scripture, we may fail to recognize our idols for what they are.

For Israel, idols were statues made of materials like wood, clay, stone, or bronze. Our modern idols are more subtle, taking the shape of anything we choose to rely on other than Christ. When we trust in it for stability, derive our significance from it, look to it to give us purpose and meaning, give up time and money to protect it, and feel anger when people challenge us over it, we may have made an idol of it.

When I ask people to name idols in the modern church, the list they come up with is often predictable: *Money. Sex. Power.* These things can be idols, but they are not the only idols of our culture. Other idols common in today's world are:

- busyness and productivity

- success

- material comfort and possessions

- fame and influence

- membership in a particular social tribe

- basing personal identity on conformity with a philosophy or lifestyle

- food—both binging on it and depriving ourselves of it

- alcohol—even if you aren't an alcoholic.

- politics and political figures

- traditions

- entertainment and distraction

- technology

- social media

What other idols would you name that are not on this list?

_____

_____

_____

Out of ignorance, Josiah and the nation of Israel may have partially fallen into the sin of idolatry. Without the full text of the law, they may not have realized how great an affront to the Lord serving other gods is. We have no such excuse. When we recognize idols in our lives, our only option is to repent and replace them with Jesus.

Pause now to search your heart. Ask God to reveal any subtle idols that have crept into your heart. If you find an idol in your life, repent. Ask God what you need to do to replace your idol with Christ.

_____

_____

_____

After purging the land of idols, Josiah led the people to celebrate Passover. Passover was the annual festival where the Jewish people celebrated their deliverance from slavery in Egypt. This festival looked back to remember how God had freed them from captivity and also anticipated how Christ would one day free us from our captivity to sin. Second Chronicles records that "the Passover had not been observed like this in Israel since the days of the prophet Samuel, and none of the kings of Israel had ever celebrated such a Passover as did Josiah" (2 Chronicles 35:18). Josiah's grandfather Hezekiah had also led the people in a great Passover celebration, but it seems Josiah's renewal of this festival eclipsed even his.

Why should celebration follow repentance?

_____

How do you think this changed life for Israel?

How can we celebrate repentance in our own lives?

How does life change for us when we cast aside our idols and return to God?

What might inspire or motivate us to make such a change?

Josiah led the people to renew the covenant with God, but Huldah's faithfulness in proclaiming God's Word inspired him to do it. Our faithfulness in proclaiming the truths of Scripture can drive both us and those around us to lay aside our idols and renew our commitments to God. Cling to God. Preach His word. That's how you leave a legacy.

NOTES

LESSON 4

THE WIDOW OF ZAREPHATH
A WOMAN FOUND BY GOD

DAY ONE

WHEN GOD FINDS YOU

A week before we got married, I lost my soon-to-be husband at the airport. First of all, you need to know that I am somewhat directionally challenged. By somewhat, I mean words like *north* and *south* are a foreign language. When people start giving me directions, all I hear is a Charlie-Brown teacher voice in my head. Ma-wah-wah-ma-wa-wa-wa. Even with the map app on my phone, I turn the wrong direction out of the parking lot about fifty percent of the time. Google's computerized "rerouting" voice often sounds deeply disappointed in me.

I'm normally able to cope with my directional difficulties, but that day at the airport threw me a curve. The plan was that I would follow Heath to the airport so he could drop off his rental car, then pick him up in front of the rental car building. Unfortunately, I overestimated my ability to drive from the back to the front of the building without getting lost. I followed him cheerfully until he pulled into the return lot, then hit my blinker to turn left and curve around to the front of the building. This was where my problem began: there were orange barrels blocking the road I wanted to take. The airport was under construction, and it seemed like there were cones or barricades blocking everywhere I wanted to turn. I drove in circles for thirty minutes, finally making my way back to the parking lot where I had left Heath. The lot was bordered by tire shredders that allowed cars in but not out, so I was afraid to pull in. I parked my car on the shoulder and cried. He finally saw me from inside the building and came out to me. "Why didn't you just pull into the drive and pick me up?" he asked. "I saw you go by at least five times." In my confusion, I hadn't realized I was actually driving by the building I was looking for. But it didn't matter—I was just grateful to be found.

It feels good to be found. Our story this week is about a woman who was found by God, maybe even before she knew she needed to be found. Yet God sought after her, and her story reminds us of God's infinite and unmatched grace. We don't know her name, only her status: a widow. Before we can meet her, though, we've got to get to know someone else: the prophet Elijah.

📖 Read 1 Kings 17:1–6.

The prophet Elijah burst on the scene during the reign of King Ahab. King Ahab has the dubious distinction of being one of Israel's most wicked kings. Ahab married Jezebel, the daughter of the king of Sidon and a devoted Baal worshiper. Ahab built an altar to Baal and led the people into Baal worship, even allowing Jezebel to murder the prophets of God. Ahab was selfish and corrupt, and he led Israel into a dark period.

God sent Elijah to Ahab with a stark message: There would be neither dew nor rain in the land until God declared it so. For Israel's agricultural society, this was a devastating pronouncement—roughly the equivalent of a prophet marching into the Oval Office and telling the president that America's supply of oil and gas would be cut off for three years. If there was no rain, there were no crops. If there were no crops, there was no food. If there was no food, people starved. Drought meant famine, starvation, and death.

This message infuriated Ahab, and he sought to kill Elijah. God hid the prophet outside the king's reach. God sent Elijah to a brook to the east of the Jordan River, outside Israel's territory. There God miraculously provided for Elijah by sending ravens to bring him bread and meat both morning and evening. Meat was a luxury in the ancient world. Having it twice a day was unheard of—only kings ate that well. God didn't just provide sustenance for Elijah. God gave him a feast.

How has God provided for you in ways that exceeded expectations?

_____

_____

_____

_____

_____

Yet Elijah's time by the brook eventually came to an end. The brook dried up because of the lack of rain, and God sent Elijah to find sustenance from another surprising source.

📖 Read 1 Kings 17:7–9.

In a time of famine, who would you think would be most likely to have food?

_____

_____

To whom did God send Elijah?

_____

God sent Elijah to find shelter with a widow. For Elijah, this command might have been as surprising as expecting ravens to bring him meat and bread. For one thing, this widow was not just any widow—this widow was a resident of Sidon, Jezebel's home turf. God was sending His prophet into the very heart of Baal's territory to shelter with the person who might be least able to aid him: a widow.

Life for widows was hard in the ancient Near East. In the best case scenario, a widow could marry again or find shelter with a member of her family. If she had no family to care for her and could not marry again, the options were typically prostitution, begging, or starvation. Because they were the poorest of the poor, God singled out widows for special protection. God strictly forbade His people from depriving widows of justice. He commanded that widows be allowed to glean from what was left in the field and said they should receive a portion of the tithe. The Psalms describe God as the "defender of widows" and the "one who sets the widow's boundary stones in place" (Psalm 68:5; Proverbs 15:25). This special protection and provision was necessary because widows often could not protect or provide for themselves.

God used two unlikely sources to provide for Elijah: first ravens, and then a widow. What did God reveal about Himself by choosing these methods to provide for Elijah?

How does this understanding help you trust God's ability to provide for you?

Even though a widow was the least likely person to be able to provide for Elijah, God intentionally sent him to this unlikely source. God's instructions were for a purpose. Verse 9 says that God had "directed" a widow to supply Elijah with food. The verb "directed" can also mean "appointed" or "commanded." This widow God sent Elijah to did not know the prophet. She was not an Israelite. She did not know the Lord. In fact, she probably worshiped Baal and the gods of Canaan just as the people around her did. Yet God chose her to provide for His prophet—and for an encounter with Himself. Elijah went to the widow because he needed food. God sent His prophet to the widow because the Lord was seeking her.

The widow reminds me that no one is outside the reach of God's grace. She was on the brink of starvation, a stranger to God and to His people, but God chose her and wove her into His story of salvation. God still does the same for us.

📖 Read Ephesians 2:14–19.

How has God sought after you?

Before we came to know Christ, we were foreigners and strangers—just like the widow. We were spiritually destitute, unable to provide salvation for ourselves. Yet through His sacrifice Christ brought us near, and made us fellow citizens with God's people and members of His household. He brought us from stranger to citizen, from scarcity to abundance, from outcast to member of the family. He knew us before we knew to look for Him and appointed us for life in His kingdom. You are here today because God is seeking you.

DAY TWO

OUR ALL-SUFFICIENT ONE

Elijah's life was in danger from King Ahab and Queen Jezebel. To keep His prophet safe, God sent Elijah to the least likely place: Jezebel's home turf. And to feed him in the midst of a famine, God sent Elijah to the least likely person: a widow.

Let's meet her.

📖 Read 1 Kings 17:7–12.

What was the widow doing when Elijah met her?

How much hope did she have?

Our widow was on the brink of starvation when her life collided with Elijah's. She was down to her last meal. Only a handful of flour and a few drops of olive oil remained in her stores. When Elijah met her, she was preparing to do the only thing she thought she could do: gather sticks to bake one last meal to feed her son, then prepare to die.

God had other plans.

I wonder what was in the widow's mind as she saw Elijah. Since she swore by Elijah's God ("As the LORD your God lives"), she must have recognized Elijah as an Israelite. It's possible she even recognized him as a prophet based on his dress and manner. He was "not from around here," and as a stranger, customs of hospitality demanded that she be courteous to him. Getting a drink for this stranger was simply being polite. Yet his second request for a piece of bread was too much for her.

I wonder what she might have been thinking:

Has this man lost his mind?

Can't he see I'm a widow?

I'm supposed to take food out of my son's mouth and give it to him?

She told Elijah as much. She and her son were going to have one last meal and then die. What emotions lay beneath her words? Anger? Fear? Despair? Scripture doesn't tell us. All we know is that she had no hope left. Yet with God, there is always hope.

Look at what Elijah said to her: "Don't be afraid. Go home and do as you have said. But first, make a small loaf of bread for me from what you have and bring it to me, and then make something for yourself and your son. For this is what the LORD, the God of Israel says: 'The jar of flour will not be used up and the jug of oil will not run dry until the day the LORD sends rain on the land' " (1 Kings 17:13–14).

Imagine being down to your last fifty dollars. You're in the grocery store parking lot about to go buy one last load of groceries to feed yourself and your family. Then a stranger walks up to you and asks you to give the money to him instead. Not only that—he promises you that his God will make sure that you and your family won't go hungry but will instead survive until the economy picks up and you get hired again. What would your thoughts be?

_____

_____

_____

What reasons can you think of that Elijah's words might have been hard for the widow to believe? List them below:

_____

_____

_____

Elijah's words defied logic. Jars of flour and oil don't replenish themselves. When every bite was precious, how could she give even a small piece of bread to a stranger instead of her son?

This God that Elijah asked her to put her faith in was not hers. Her first words to Elijah make that clear: "As the LORD *your* God lives" (emphasis added). This God Elijah knew might be powerful—but He was not a god she knew. The Lord was Israel's God, and she was no Israelite. Worshiping many gods was common in the ancient Near East. Adopting a new deity wouldn't have been a problem for her. Yet believing that this God could and would actually do something for her? That was another matter. In the ancient world, many people thought of gods as being local. The God of Israel had no reason to care about a Sidonian widow, and she had no reason to think that this unknown God had any power outside His nation's borders. Elijah asked her to ignore everything she knew and put her faith in a God she didn't know—a God she had no reason to believe could and would care about her. She had every reason to turn her back and walk away.

But she did what Elijah had said.

Think for a moment about all the places our widow could have second-guessed herself and turned back. On the walk to her home. As she poured out her last dregs of flour and drops of oil. As she kneaded the scarce dough and divided it into impossibly small loaves of bread. As she slid the tiny loaves into the oven. As she carried them out to Elijah and placed one in the prophet's hand. Did she stop and wonder what she was doing? Consider if she was only condemning her son to die sooner? Or did she find a tiny glimmer of hope—enough to follow through on what must have seemed like an impossible plan?

I don't know where she found the faith. In her shoes, I don't know if I would have had the courage to do the same. Yet something in Elijah's words kindled a flame of hope. It was enough to nurture one small seed of faith, and she acted on God's promise. That tiny seed of faith was enough. "So there was food every day for Elijah and for the woman and her family. For the jar of flour was not used up and the jug of oil did not run dry, in keeping with the word of the LORD spoken by Elijah" (1 Kings 17:15–16).

What do you think the widow learned about God from this experience?

_____

_____

How does her story speak to you?

_____

_____

_____

Here's what I know: God's grace is enough. God is not limited by geography, economics, or ethnicity. It doesn't matter how much food you have in your pantry or dollars in your bank account. God is the All-Sufficient One.

His forgiveness is enough for our sin.

His strength is enough for our frailty.

His healing is enough for our brokenness.

His deliverance is enough for our bondage.

His provision is enough for our need.

How do you need God to be enough for you today?

_____

_____

_____

Today, put your trust in our all-sufficient God. Commit your needs to God and express your trust that He will meet them. Write out your prayer in the space below and ask God to be your enough today.

_____

_____

_____

_____

_____

_____

DAY THREE

OUR ALL-SUFFICIENT ONE

Several years ago I went through a crisis of faith. A friend of ours, a young father, died. It tore me apart. On one level, I didn't feel like I had the right to grieve. I still had my husband. On another level, I was wrestling with questions of why God hadn't answered our prayers the way I wanted Him to.

My downward spiral deepened after we visited Mrs. Bee in the nursing home. Even in her nineties, Mrs. Bee was vibrant. She gardened everyday and always had cookies for our toddler when she visited. She knew Jesus would take her home one day, and I half expected that one day her neighbor would find her in the garden, hoe in her hand and heaven on her face.

But that didn't happen. Our family relocated, and we didn't see Mrs. Bee for over a year. During that time, she moved to a nursing home. When we saw her after our friend's death, I almost didn't recognize her. She was curled into a wheelchair like a shrunken doll. There was no spark in her eyes—no sign she recognized us. The staff kept a pressure sensor on her bed and strapped her into her chair so she wouldn't get up without assistance. She didn't speak, even when my daughter sang her favorite song.

We left, and my anger grew with every slap of my sandals against the parking lot asphalt. This wasn't the life—or the death—Mrs. Bee had wanted. If she could have chosen, she would have gladly been in heaven instead of living this shadow existence. And if he could have chosen, our friend would have been home with his children, healthy and whole. Why had God allowed her to live like this and our friend to die? _God,_ I thought. _I know you are good. But this is not right._

There are moments when the truth of our faith clashes with the reality of our experience. In those moments it produces a crisis of faith: Do we really believe what we say is true?

Are we willing to hold on to our faith in the unknown, to live with the tension of our questions and uncertainty, trusting God's sovereignty even when it hurts? When the lights go out and you're alone in the darkness, will you still believe?

The widow of Zarephath's fledgling faith faced a fierce storm. Yet her desperation brought her face to face with God's deliverance.

Let's see what happened.

📖 Read 1 Kings 17:17–18.

How did the widow's experience clash with her knowledge of God?

_____

_____

What beliefs about God did her cry reveal?

_____

_____

Can you relate to the widow's crisis of faith? How have your experiences come into conflict with your knowledge of God? How did that affect you?

_____

_____

_____

We don't know how long Elijah was in the widow's home, but it seems to have been for some period of time. Perhaps a year—maybe even two. Remember, the widow did not know God before she met Elijah. Feeding the prophet her last crumbs of food was her first act of faith.

Scripture doesn't fill in the details of the weeks or months Elijah spent with the widow. It's a story where my imagination wants to fill in the gaps. Elijah doesn't seem the type to keep quiet about God. During his stay in the widow's home, did Elijah tell her and her son God's great story of salvation? Did he tell her about how God called Abraham to a land he did not know, about Moses and the burning bush and the miraculous parting of the Red Sea? Did he tell her about how God provided manna in the wilderness and how Jericho's walls fell down but Rahab's house stood firm? Did he tell her about another foreign widow—Ruth—and how she became the great-grandmother of Israel's greatest king?

Surely he told her these stories, and perhaps more. And surely day by day as the empty jar continued to yield flour and the empty jug continued to pour out oil, the tiny kernel of faith the widow had found began to grow and bloom a fragile flower.

Then tragedy struck. The widow's son grew sick. Did she hold on to faith even in that moment? Surely the God who had fed her and His prophet would not allow this child he had saved from starvation to die. Yet he grew worse and weaker. And then, with her son's final gasping breath, the widow broke:

> *"What do you have against me, man of God? Did you come to*
> *remind me of my sin and kill my son?" (1 Kings 17:18)*

Can you hear the anguish in her cry? Heartbroken grief at her son's death, but also betrayal and pain. She had done what this strange, unknown God had asked of her, and He had taken the most precious thing she had. In her worldview, a tragedy like this meant the gods were to blame—and the closest God at hand was the one whose prophet had been living in her home. So in her anger, she lashed out at God and the prophet He had sent.

Did you come to kill my son?

Crises of faith strip us bare, exposing the cracks in our faith foundation. For the widow, it was that she had thought of God the same way as the deities her people worshiped—capricious and cruel. The ancient gods often treated people as nuisances and slaves. If good things happened, they were pleased with you. If bad things happened, the gods were angry at you. If the gods were angry at you, you had done something wrong and needed to make a sacrifice or perform the right rituals to make them pleased with you again.

We might shake our heads and wonder how anyone could live that way, but the truth is that we often have our own false beliefs about God. Often we don't recognize the hollowness of these false beliefs until something exposes them—something like a crisis of faith.

We don't always put words to our false beliefs, but if we did they might go something like this:

If I don't perform and achieve, God won't be pleased with me.

Jesus' sacrifice was great, but to really be saved I have to prove I deserve it.

I will never be good enough.

I don't deserve for God to hear my prayers.

If something bad happens in my life, it's because God is punishing me.

I can't fully trust God because if I'm not in control, something bad will happen.

If God was really good, this pain in my life wouldn't be happening.

The danger of these false beliefs is that belief leads to action. If we believe our salvation depends on our performance, we can't enjoy the gracious rest God has provided for us. If we believe God is out to get us, we miss the freedom and intimacy of a relationship with God. If we believe it's up to us to hold our worlds together, we set ourselves up for stress, heartbreak, and failure.

For me, my crisis of faith exposed an unwillingness to live with mystery and uncertainty. I wanted faith to make sense. It was one thing to talk about trusting God's heart when you can't see His hand. It was another thing to live it. At the bottom of it, I had failed to trust God's sovereignty. I wanted God to do what I wanted, how and when I wanted it done.

God doesn't work that way. Yet for months, I let my anger and frustration drive me from God. The idol I had built up in my mind was of a tame God who only acted in ways that made sense to me. My questions and doubts smashed into that futile idol and brought its clay feet crashing down. I needed to fully embrace God's sovereignty and to find a faith that was willing to trust God even when my questions went unanswered. Not uncritically or unthinkingly—I believe God gave us our brains for a reason. Yet there are things we may never fully understand this side of heaven. In those places of darkness, there are times when we need to simply trust in God's light. My pain does not alter God's goodness. My questions do not erase God's wisdom. And my fear does not shift God's power. God is God, and faith sometimes requires us to live with the unknowing.

The experience awakened me anew to God's grace. God doesn't turn away from our grief and pain. He is not surprised by our doubt or caught off guard by our anger. When our soul cries out "Why?", God is there to embrace us in the midst of our questioning. He sits with us in our pain, holds us in our agony, and comforts us in our grief. We may not get the answers to our questions, but we often find that God's presence is the only answer we need. When we walk through the valley of death, resurrection waits on the other side.

That's what the widow was about to find out.

Today, I invite you to linger in an unhurried time with God. Maybe this lesson finds you raw and hurting. If so, let God minister to you with His peace. Maybe you are wrestling with your own crisis of faith. If that's you, ask God to expose any false beliefs you hold and draw them into the light so they can be healed. And if you are at peace and life is good, thank God for His faithfulness. Ask God to continue to lead you into the truth of who He is. Use the space below to journal your thoughts. And stay tuned—tomorrow we're going to discover the depths of God's deliverance. When God is with us, we are never alone.

DAY FOUR

OUR GOD OF TRUTH

Yesterday we left the widow in the middle of her darkest moment. Little did she know the sun was rising. Hope was on the way.

📖 Read 1 Kings 17:19–24. How did God deliver hope for the widow?

Put yourself in Elijah's shoes for a moment. As we saw yesterday, the widow didn't know God's character. Elijah did. Elijah knew that the Lord, not Baal, was the one true God. He knew that God controlled life and death. And he knew that the God who had sent ravens to feed him and kept the widow's supply of oil and flour flowing had not sent him to her to bring death. He served a God of life. And so Elijah prayed an audacious prayer: that God would return life to the widow's son.

Praying that God would raise the dead is a bold prayer under any circumstances. It was even more so for Elijah. At this point in salvation history, no one had been raised from the dead before. Abraham, Moses, David—all the heroes of faith in Israel's story—had never dared ask God for something so bold. Death was the end. Final. But Elijah refused to believe that God intended the widow's story to end this way, and he begged God to return life to the widow's son.

God answered. The boy lived.

Miracles in Scripture are always for a purpose. They are in a sense enacted parables, a story that tells a truth about who God is.

When God raised the widow's son from the dead, what truth did that miracle tell about who God is?

How is that truth important to you?

The overarching conflict in the Elijah stories is the question of whether the Lord or Baal was the one true God. Elijah believed God was. Jezebel and her prophets believed Baal was. The people of Israel had to choose whom they would serve. The widow's story was a trumpet blast announcing God's sovereignty and power. God had usurped a power Baal claimed—the power to give and withhold rain. At a time when most people thought of gods as regional deities whose power stopped at their nation's borders, God had sent His prophet into the heart of Baal's territory and shown that He had the power to provide both for His prophet even there. Where Baal took and demanded, God showed that He gave and cared for the most vulnerable. And now, God proved that He alone held the power over life and death. The Lord was and is the one true God.

> *Elijah picked up the child and carried him down from the room into the house. He gave him to his mother and said, "Look, your son is alive!*

Then the woman said to Elijah. "Now I know that you are a man of
God and that the word of the LORD from your mouth is the truth"
(1 Kings 17:24).

What does it mean to know that the word of the Lord is truth?

What convinced the widow that what Elijah said about God was true?

How do you know that the word of God is true?

The widow's experience of God's life-giving power irrevocably convinced her that what Elijah had said about God was true. God had given her son life. She knew it. She had seen it. She had lived it. And with that, she put her faith fully in the Lord, giving God her undivided allegiance.

God still demands our undivided allegiance. Our choice is not between God and Baal, but we are still tempted by the idols of our culture. Our world screams at us to put our trust in the gods it chooses:

Idolatry of self: I determine what is true or right for me. Salvation comes from fulfilling and being true to myself.

Idolatry of effort: My value comes in what I do and achieve. What I work for is good; those who do not work the way I think they should deserve shame. Salvation comes when I earn it.

Idolatry of tribe: My tribe and community determines what is right and true. If my tribe says it, I believe it. Other tribes are the enemy, and anything they say is false, dangerous, and should be mocked. I am saved when my tribe wins.

Idolatry of wealth: Those who have wealth are righteous. I purchase salvation by accumulating money and possessions for myself.

These idols lure us, promising an easier way to salvation than yielding to Christ's authority. They whisper that we don't really need to die to self; that we can cling to our self-deceptions and still have it all. But the stench of death clings to them. Christ alone brings life. And to follow Him, we must recognize that He is truth.

📖 Read John 14:6. Who is Jesus?

How do you know Jesus' words are true?

The widow believed because God demonstrated His life-giving power to her. Few of us will ever see anyone raised from the dead. Yet God still invites us to be witnesses of His power.

The apostle John wrote to the church at Ephesus about his eyewitness experience of Jesus:

> *That which was from the beginning, which we have heard, which we have seen with our eyes, which we have looked at and our hands have touched—this we proclaim concerning the way of life. (1 John 1:1)*

Underline the verbs—the action words—in the verse above.

How did John know that what he preached about Jesus was true?

We have not seen Jesus with our lives, heard His audible voice, or touched His physical body, but our experience with the risen Christ is still experience with Jesus.

What have you heard about Jesus?

Where have you seen Christ at work in your life?

How has God's presence been tangible to you? How have you touched the reality of Christ's presence?

_____

_____

_____

What do you proclaim concerning the way of life?

_____

_____

_____

The idols of our culture may glisten, but the truth of God's word reveals them for the weak, powerless things they are. Jesus is our only hope for salvation. Jesus holds life and death in His hands. Jesus' word is truth, and when chaos swirls around us we need to cling even tighter to Him. We are witnesses to the power of God at work in and through us. Like the widow, we must testify to what we have seen.

What will you testify about Jesus this week? Write out your thoughts in the space below:

_____

_____

_____

_____

_____

_____

DAY FIVE

WHO TELLS YOUR STORY?

One of my favorite moments from the *Hamilton* musical comes at the end. In the musical's closing song, Alexander Hamilton's widow, Eliza, steps into the spotlight and sings about how she told her husband's story. This part of the musical is based on fact. Many of the founding fathers were able to shape their own narratives through the lengthy memoirs and autobiographies they left behind. Hamilton, killed at age 49 in a duel with former vice-president Aaron Burr, did not have time to cement his own legacy. Eliza did it for him. Eliza lived another fifty years after her husband's death. She founded an orphanage, established a school, continued to support the abolitionist movement, opened her home to slave children from the neighborhood, and helped raise funds for the Washington Monument. She also worked tirelessly to secure her husband's legacy, interviewing soldiers and politicians who had served with her husband, collecting letters Hamilton had written to Washington from Mount Vernon, and eventually enlisting her son to write a massive biography of her husband. Some details of Hamilton's life, such as his role in ghostwriting Washington's final address, we know because Eliza found ways to tell her husband's story.[9]

It matters who tells your story. One of the reasons we know about the widow of Zarephath is that Jesus told her story.

Jesus told the story of the widow of Zarephath on His final visit to Nazareth, His hometown. Jesus began His public ministry in Galilee, the northern region of Israel. He preached in the synagogues throughout the region and performed many miracles. Word about Him quickly spread.

Then Jesus returned to preach in Nazareth, His hometown (Luke 4:14–30). The crowd treated Him with honor and invited Him to read from the law. Jesus read a passage from Isaiah that describes the coming of the Messiah, Israel's promised savior. Jesus announced that these words had been fulfilled that day in their hearing.

Initially the crowd spoke well of Jesus. But Jesus also knew what was in their hearts, and He challenged their presumption.

📖 Read Luke 4:23–27.

Why do you think the crowd wanted Jesus to do in their hometown what He had done in Capernaum?

Jesus responded to the crowd's unspoken demand by mentioning times God showed grace to two foreigners—the widow of Zarephath and Naaman, a Syrian general who God healed of leprosy. Why might Jesus have emphasized these two stories?

When Israel was birthed as a people, God called them to be a "kingdom of priests and a holy nation" (Exodus 19:6). As priests represented God to the people and the people to God, so Israel was meant to stand as a light to the nations. God chose Israel as His special possession, but God also wanted the rest of the world to know Him. Yet Israel thought that being God's special possession made God their possession as well. Though there were converts at times—such as Rahab, Ruth, Naaman, and the widow of Zarephath—these stories are scattered far and few between throughout the Old Testament. Rather than being a light for the nations, through most of their history Israel kept the light for themselves.

This helps explain the attitude of Jesus's hometown neighbors when He entered the synagogue. Nazareth was a primarily Jewish community. Galilee, where Jesus had begun His ministry, had a mix of both Jews and Gentiles. It seems that the people of Nazareth were disgruntled that Jesus had begun His ministry somewhere else. They thought they were entitled to see Jesus do the same miracles for them that He had done elsewhere.

Why is a sense of spiritual entitlement dangerous? What misunderstanding about our relationship with God does spiritual entitlement reveal?

Jesus reminded the crowd about Naaman and the widow of Zarephath to remind them that God's grace did not stop at Israel's borders. As we've seen, God could have sent Elijah to any number of widows inside Israel—widows who were just as desperate and alone as our widow was. But God sent Elijah to her. God was seeking her. Yet God also sought her to tell part of His story—a story of salvation that is not limited to language, race, or tribe. God meant to show that His power had no limits; that He alone was and is the sovereign God, and that His salvation is meant for all peoples.

Including a Syrian widow.

Including you.

Including me.

That is good news for us—but it sounded like bad news to the people of Nazareth. They were so outraged by Jesus's suggestion that God had sent the Messiah to outsiders and foreigners, that they drove Him out of town and tried to throw Jesus off a cliff. Jesus simply walked through the crowd and went on His way. The gospel of Luke does not record that Jesus ever returned to Nazareth again.

Reflect on that tragedy. How could a group of people be so angry about Jesus' desire to welcome others that they failed to welcome Him? What warning does this story hold for us?

God loves outsiders. That should be a great comfort to us because we have all felt like we were on the outside looking in. Yet it should also be a warning. Like the people of Nazareth, we can easily slip into the sin of spiritual entitlement. We can start believing that having a personal relationship with God means that God is our personal possession. We can forget that when God said to take the gospel to all people, God really meant all.

Even the people we don't like.

Even the people we are afraid of.

Even the people we disagree with.

Even the people we think are enemies.

Even those we secretly think are outside the reach of God's grace.

This is a place we need to do some deep soul searching. The spiritual answers are easy. *Of course* we believe Jesus died to save all people. *Of course* we believe God's grace is sufficient. But sometimes we start singing a different tune when someone enters our church that doesn't quite fit in. They ask uncomfortable questions. Their politics are different. They haven't learned the rules of acceptable church behavior. They're from a group we instinctively see with suspicion or even prejudice. And then, when they drift away after attending for a few weeks, we shrug our shoulders and say "Well, what did you expect?"

Has there ever been anyone you have acted as if God could not save?

_____

_____

God is less concerned with our heritage than our humility. At a time when God's people had abandoned Him for other gods, the Lord found faith in a Syrian widow. She wasn't part of Israel, but she was still a person God had chosen. When God gave her an invitation to believe, she responded.

God gave that same invitation to the people of Nazareth. Jesus, the Messiah they had waited for, was right there in front of them. He told them directly He was the one the prophets had promised, the one their salvation and hope depended on. But their arrogance and entitlement blinded them. They were so focused on what God should do that they missed what He was doing. Their pride not only caused them to reject Jesus—it caused them to try to murder Him.

How can pride cause us to reject the work of God in our lives?

_____

_____

Have you ever been guilty of this?

_____

_____

We will not leave a legacy of faith if we try to dictate to God what He should do and should not do. It is not for us to determine who is worthy of God's grace. Truth is, none of us are. That's what makes it grace.

To leave a legacy of faith, we need to take a lesson from the widow of Zarephath. Let go of expectation and embrace the freedom of God's sovereignty. Walk in dependence on the Lord, believing that His well of grace never runs dry. Know that the Lord alone is God, and trust Him alone. And remember, no one is beyond the limits of God's grace—even you.

He has found you. God is writing your story—and it's going to be amazing. Put your trust in Him.

LESSON 5

LEAH
CHOOSING CHRIST OVER COMPETITION

DAY ONE

A TALE OF TWO SISTERS

My first taste of rejection was in college. I had applied for a position that seemed perfect for me and one I desperately wanted. It fit in with my dreams of the future, and I was convinced it was God's will for me. I aced the interview and had solid recommendations. I just knew the job was mine.

But I didn't get the position. In the end, the committee chose someone else. It sent me into a tailspin of questioning myself and my ability to hear from God. In the end things worked out for the best, but for a period of time my self-doubt throbbed like a broken bone.

Rejection hurts. Whether we are passed over for an invitation, a date, a promotion, or an opportunity, it hurts to not be the one chosen. And when another person is consistently chosen or favored over us, it's hard not to let resentment, hurt, and a spirit of competition set in.

Describe a time you felt rejected or passed over.

_____

_____

_____

_____

How did you deal with the pain?

_____

_____

_____

This week we're going to meet a woman who was unchosen and unwanted, constantly living in her sister's shadow. Yet God chose her to be the mother of priests and kings, and she teaches us about the power of choosing our own legacy.

Let's meet Leah.

📖 Read Genesis 29:16–17.

How does the text describe Leah?

_____

_____

How does it describe her sister, Rachel?

_____

_____

What conclusions can you draw from the two descriptions?

_____

_____

_____

There's some ambiguity about the way Genesis describes Leah. Some translations read that she had "lovely eyes." Others read that she had "weak eyes." Either is a possibility, but the Bible makes it clear that Leah paled in comparison to her younger sister, Rachel. Rachel "had a lovely figure and was beautiful" (Genesis 29:17). Perhaps Leah's eyes were her one good feature. Or perhaps she was extremely nearsighted, limiting her ability to cope in a world without glasses, contacts, or other forms of visual correction. Either way, we know that the younger sister outshone the elder—something that often doesn't bode well for sibling relationships.

Things got more complicated for Rachel and Leah when Jacob entered the picture. Jacob was the son of Isaac, the grandson of Abraham. Jacob's name means "trickster," and he proved himself worthy of his name. Though Jacob was the younger son, he convinced Esau, his older brother, to sell Jacob his birthright for a bowl of stew. When Isaac grew old, Jacob deceived his blind father into thinking he was Esau. Jacob stole the blessing intended for his elder brother. Esau was incensed and vowed to kill Jacob. Jacob's mother sent him back to her homeland to take shelter with her brother, Laban.

Jacob is not much of a hero at this point in the story. His one redeeming quality is that he valued the inheritance Esau had despised. Yet God showed Jacob grace he did not deserve. God promised Jacob that He had chosen him to inherit the promise first shown to Abraham. It would be Jacob who would inherit the land; Jacob whose descendants would fill the earth; Jacob through whom all nations of the earth would be blessed. God promised Jacob that the Lord would be with him on this long journey and that God would bring him back home.

Jacob pledged his loyalty and service to God there in the wilderness. He continued his journey on to Paddan-Aram, his mother's home. Once he arrived, he began looking for Laban. The first member of the family he met was Laban's youngest daughter, Rachel. Jacob seems to have fallen in love with Rachel almost on sight.

📖 Read Genesis 29:18–20.

How would you describe Jacob's love for Rachel?

Jacob quickly decided he wanted Rachel for his wife, and her father agreed. The wedding, however, did not go according to plan.

📖 Read Genesis 29:19–30

What trick did Laban play on Jacob? How do you think Rachel felt about the situation?

How did you think Leah felt?

Scripture doesn't always give us the details we would like. Some scholars think Leah was complicit in Laban's scheme. Others think she was simply a pawn in her father's attempt to get free labor out of Jacob. Regardless of her feelings on the matter, I doubt Leah had a choice in the matter. There's a world of heartbreak in these short verses. Leah had a week with her new husband, and then Rachel became Jacob's second wife. "And his love for Rachel was greater than his love for Leah" (Genesis 29:30).

There's a lot we don't know in this passage. In a culture where polygamy was accepted, were the sisters happy to be married to the same man? Or had Leah looked forward to marriage as an escape from her younger sister's shadow, only to find herself now more trapped than before? Again, Scripture doesn't tell us—although the competition that springs up between the two sisters indicates all was not bliss in Jacob's home.

What we do know is that Jacob did not treat Leah fairly. As Jacob's first wife, under the societal norms of the day she should have been entitled to a higher position and privilege than Rachel. But Jacob clearly loved Rachel more. Under Old Testament law, a husband who took a second wife was not to deny the rights of the first wife (Exodus 21:10–11). Jacob's favoritism of Rachel was unfair to Leah and set the stage for conflict between the two sisters.

And so Leah enters the story as unlovely and unloved. She was married to a husband who had to be tricked into marrying her and who loved her sister more. Did she cry herself to sleep at night? Was there anyone there to see?

When have you felt the most isolated and alone?

_____

_____

_____

What comforts you the most when you feel rejected and hurt?

_____

_____

Leah may have felt alone in her struggles. We don't have to be. There is no struggle or pain we face that Jesus doesn't understand. We will all feel rejected and alone. So did Jesus.

📖 Read at least two of the following passages:

Isaiah 52:2–3   Mark 14:43, 50–52   Luke 23:13–24

John 8:58–59   Luke 22:54–62

When you feel rejected, how do you know Jesus understands your pain?

_____

_____

When people rejected Jesus, did their rejection of Him say anything about how God loved, valued, and accepted Him?

_____

_____

Does people's rejection of you change anything about the way God loves, values, and accepts you?

_____

_____

People may have rejected Jesus, but God did not. Jesus is "the living Stone—rejected by humans but chosen by God and precious to him" (1 Peter 2:4). As the Old Testament prophesied, "The stone the builders rejected has become the cornerstone" (Psalm 118:22; 1 Peter 2:7). Though the people rejected Jesus as the Messiah, God's promised deliverer, God chose Him as the cornerstone of His kingdom, the one piece upon which the whole structure depended and which held the entire building together. People rejected Jesus, but their rejection did not alter God's purpose for Him.

God's purposes for you are not altered either when people reject you. You are adopted, chosen, and beloved. You are seen. I'm sure there were days when Leah felt invisible and small. Yet her circumstances did not alter God's character, and God was working behind the scenes on her behalf. We'll see more of that story tomorrow. But for today, know that you are not alone. God sees. God knows. God cares. And when others say there's no place for you, know that God has already pulled up a chair for you at the table. You are welcomed in His home and in His heart. With Him there is acceptance and love.

DAY TWO

UNLOVED, BUT NOT UNSEEN

Leah was unloved by her husband, but she was not unseen. Her story has a lightning ray of hope:

> *"When the Lord saw that Leah was not loved . . . " (Genesis 29:31).*

Who saw that Leah was not loved?

What difference does it make that God saw that she was unloved?

God, the maker of heaven and earth, saw that Leah was unloved. Jacob perhaps regarded her as unlovely and unloveable, but God didn't. God saw her. And in Scripture, when God sees something, God acts on it.

God saw that the world that He had made was good, and God was pleased with His creation (Genesis 1:31).

God saw that people had become wicked and corrupt, and God warned Noah that He would send a flood (Genesis 6:11–13).

God saw the misery of His people's slavery in Egypt, and He sent Moses to deliver them (Exodus 3:7–10).

Jesus saw the faith of four friends who brought a paralyzed man to Jesus, and He healed the man (Mark 2:5).

Jesus saw a woman who had been bleeding for four years. He told her that her faith had made her well (Matthew 9:20–22)

When Jesus saw a large crowd, He had compassion on them and taught them (Mark 6:34).

A God who sees is a God prepared to act. God saw Leah's pain, and He was prepared to act on her behalf.

How has God acted on your behalf in response to your pain?

How does it encourage you to know that God sees you?

God saw that Leah was unloved, and God responded by blessing Leah with children.

📖 Read Genesis 29:31–32

What did Leah name her son and why?

What did she hope would be the result of her son's birth?

Biblical names often carry meaning. The name of Leah's first son, Reuben, is a double word play. Literally it means, "see, a son," but Reuben also sounds like the Hebrew for "He has seen my misery." Leah understood that God had seen her misery. She recognized her son as the gift from God he was, and yet she still was focused on her longing for Jacob's love.

DID YOU KNOW?
Significance in Names

In Scripture, names often carry meaning. Names may say something about a person's relationship with God, the person's character, or the person's destiny. Some examples of biblical names with significant meanings are Abraham, "father of nations," Jacob, "trickster," and Joshua, "The LORD is my salvation." Leah named her children based on her hopes for her relationship with Jacob and her relationship with God.

Leah is not alone in her craving for love. Years ago I worked in a school district that had one of the highest teen pregnancy rates in our state. Several high school students on my roll were pregnant or had infants. One of these young women shared with me why she had gotten pregnant. "I got pregnant on purpose," she said. "I wanted someone who would love me all the time."

I ached for her because I knew the baby she wanted wouldn't satisfy her soul-hunger. No person can. Our friends, children, spouses, and families are gifts from God that we should cherish, but they cannot make us whole. If we look to them to satisfy the cravings of our soul, we are doomed to disappointment. People cannot do for us what only Christ can do. It's not fair to them for us to expect them to, because no person can be Jesus to us. Trying to put another person in Christ's place sets us up for heartbreak. That person we think will satisfy the hunger of our hearts, who will make us feel loved, and who will finally make us complete— is only a flawed, sinful human being just like we are. Eventually they will fail us.

When the people we have placed our hopes upon let us down, we start looking for another way to heal our pain. Sometimes we reject the person who hurt us, falling for the deception that there must be someone out there better who can make us whole. Sometimes we try to fix the person, thinking if we can change them they will be able to satisfy the longings of our hearts. Sometimes we wind up repeating the cycle of unrealistic expectation and hurt. We unconsciously try to recreate the broken patterns of relationships where we have been wounded, thinking this time we'll be able to get it right.

It never works. What we need is not another person. What we need is a perfect Savior. Only Christ can satisfy the longings of our hearts.

How have you tried to satisfy your craving for love apart from Christ? Why did those efforts fail you?

Leah had to learn the same painful lesson. It took time.

God gave Leah a second son:

> She said "Because the Lord heard that I am not loved, he gave me this one too." So she named him Simeon. Again she concieved, and

when she gave birth to a son she said, "Now at last my husband will become attached to me, because I have borne him three sons." So he was named Levi. She conceived again, and when she gave birth to a son she said, "This time I will praise the Lord." So she named him Judah. (Genesis 29:33–35)

Go back to the passage above and circle the names Leah gave her children. Underline the comments she made after each child was born. What progression or shift do you see in her thinking?

_____

_____

Leah began her marriage with a hunger for love. With each child that was born, she hoped that this time her husband would love her. Yet nothing seemed to shift in her relationship with Jacob. After Judah was born, her comments were different. "This time," Leah said, "I will praise the LORD."

How would you explain the shift in Leah's thinking after Judah's birth? Why had her perspective changed?

_____

_____

I want to pause here to point out how long Leah's journey was. She had four children, so there were at least four years from Reuben's birth to Judah's. It was probably longer than that, though. If Leah nursed the children herself, this would have spaced out her pregnancies. These two verses likely cover a time period of eight to ten long years when Leah hungered for love that her husband would not give her. Yet at the end, she seems to have found contentment. We have no indication that Leah's relationship with Jacob changed. But her relationship with God did. Despite her heartbreak, Leah chose to praise the Lord.

When we are heartsick and soul-worn, sometimes that's all we need to do: look up. We don't look to a person or a program or anything else that promises to fill us. We look up to the Savior who was lifted high on a cross for us. These soul hungers we think are a longing to be loved, to achieve, to belong, or to be filled, are there to point us to the only one who can satisfy our soul: Jesus. He is the Savior who died so that we could be made whole. When we hunger for Him, we find ourselves satisfied. The desires of our hearts are met when Christ is our foremost desire. If we are soul hungry it is not that we have wanted too much—it is that we have attempted to satisfy ourselves with too little. Jesus is what we need. When Christ meets our need, our only possible response is to praise Him.

Today spend time before the Lord examining the longings of your heart. What is the brass ring you've been chasing? Have you tried to feed yourself on something less than

Christ, only to find yourself hungrier than before? Identify your soul hunger today. Run your hands around it and find the edges. Put a name to it. Then set it before the throne of God and ask Him to fill it as only He can. Ask God to show you clearly, specifically, and scripturally how Jesus can meet that need. He will. And when He does, praise His name!

DAY THREE

CHECKING A COMPETITIVE SPIRIT

Patterns are hard to break. One of my ongoing struggles has been taming my sweet tooth. I want to eat nutritious foods that are good for my body. I also really like chocolate. When I'm tired, hungry, having a bad day, or want to treat myself, I reach for the candy bowl. It's a habit, a pattern. I've gotten better at putting boundaries around my eating and filling myself up on healthy foods. Yet that ingrained pattern is still there, like the impression left on a legal pad when you tear the top page off. When I'm stressed, tired, or have a weak moment, it's still very easy for me to turn back to the pattern of using sweets for comfort. I'm learning to counter those weak moments with intentionality and prayer. I'm also learning how to indulge within limits, not letting a treat become a binge. I hope in time my new patterns will replace the old.

That's the trouble with patterns. They become a default response that we unthinkingly return to time and time again. When we train ourselves in healthy habits, that training automaticity can work in our favor. Yet when our patterns are unhealthy, it takes time and effort to train ourselves in new habits and ways of thinking. Sometimes these patterns are benign. We take the same route to work every day, load the dishwasher from front to back instead of back to front, or put on our pants right leg first instead of left. Sometimes though, these patterns are more complex. We have patterns that are formed in us for how we handle money, how we respond to conflict, how we steward our time, and how we nurture our relationships. Changing these ingrained patterns can be hard. Even when we have changed them, sometimes we find ourselves slipping back into old patterns.

What patterns have you struggled to change or break? What makes changing these so hard?

Leah also found herself trapped in a pattern that was hard to change: competition with her sister. She found a new perspective in her relationship with God, but she still found that changing the dynamics of her relationship with Rachel was challenging.

📖 Read Genesis 30:1–12

What was the source of tension between the two sisters?

How did Rachel respond?

What do the names of Rachel's children indicate about her motivations?

What did Leah do in response?

Infertility is a painful struggle in any generation. In the ancient world, infertility was a great cause of anguish for women. A woman's job was to have children. If a woman could not have children, she lost status and value in the eyes of her husband and her community. An infertile wife was sufficient reason for a husband to take a second wife. It could also justify divorce. Rachel was a beloved beauty, but her infertility was a personal tragedy.

When Jacob's mother had been unable to conceive, his father prayed for her, and God blessed them with children. Unlike his father, Jacob blamed God for Rachel's infertility. Rachel looked for her own solution.

The answer Rachel landed on was giving one of her slaves to Jacob to serve as a surrogate for her. To us, this might read as exploitation. In Rachel's world, however, this was a culturally acceptable solution. Jacob's grandmother, Sarah, had taken similar actions to cope with her infertility. Some ancient marriage contracts specify that the wife could have a slave act as surrogate for her if she was unable to conceive.[10] Rachel's actions were in accordance with the morality and culture of her time.

Her plan worked. Rachel's slave, Bilhah, had two sons. But now Leah had stopped having children. Her ability to conceive had been the one thing giving her leverage over her younger, beautiful, more beloved sister. And this is where Leah's old patterns began to raise their ugly heads. Whatever progress she had made in looking to God for acceptance instead of Jacob began to erode as fear of losing place to her sister crept back in. She took a page out of Rachel's playbook. She took her slave, Zilpah, and gave her to Jacob as a surrogate. Zilpah bore Leah two sons.

How would you describe the relationship between Rachel and Leah at this point?

Describe a time you were in competition with someone. How did it affect your relationship?

Competition can be healthy when it spurs us to excellence. That wasn't the case with Rachel and Leah, though. The two sisters were competing for Jacob's love, and the competition poisoned their relationships.

📖 Read Genesis 30:14–23.

How did the competition between Rachel and Leah continue to affect their relationship with one another and with Jacob?

Mandrakes were a plant with a forked root that people believed could enhance fertility. The relationship between Rachel, Leah, and Jacob had become so twisted by the sisters' competition with one another that Leah purchased a night with her husband from Rachel with the mandrakes her son had found. Jacob's affection had become a commodity the sisters thought they could buy and sell. In their race to outdo one another, they had lost sight of the true value and importance of their relationships.

That's one of the dangers of competition. An attitude of competition is founded on a belief in scarcity. Rachel and Leah lived as if each other's success threatened her own. We can do the same thing. Instead of being happy when those around us succeed, we can grow resentful and begin to doubt ourselves.

I dealt with this in a small way while pitching a book proposal. We had sent the proposal around to several publishers, and, one after another, they all turned it down. At the same time, I was seeing friends and colleagues signing contracts and winning awards. It was hard celebrating their successes in a time when every door I knocked on was closed. I started becoming critical, finding details to nitpick in other people's messages or platforms. I complained to my husband about how unfair it all was.

God brought me up short with a message Jesus gave His disciples about the danger of a competitive spirit. One day James and John, two brothers who were among Jesus' twelve disciples, came to Jesus and asked Him to let one of them sit on His right and one on His left. They were asking that when Jesus came into His power, that He would give them the two positions of greatest honor and authority. When the other disciples found out, they were outraged.

Jesus challenged their competitive spirits:

> *"You know that those who are regarded as rulers of the Gentiles lord*
> *it over them, and their high officials exercise authority over them.*
> *Not so with you. Instead, whoever wants to become great among you*
> *must be your servant, and whoever wants to be first must be slave of*
> *all. For even the Son of Man did not come to be served, but to serve,*
> *and to give his life as a ransom for many." (Mark 10:42)*

In the kingdom of God, how do we become great?

How do Jesus' words in this passage speak to us about living with a spirit of competition?

I had to learn that honor is not a limited commodity. A friend's success does not limit mine, and if God chooses to honor someone else it does not mean that my honor diminishes. The body of Christ is not a competition where some are more valuable than another. Jesus did not come to be served but to serve and to give Himself in sacrifice. We are meant to follow His example. Our goal is not status, but service. We don't have to compete with each other because our personal renown is not the end goal. Christ's name deserves praise, not our own. We can rejoice whenever God receives glory—no matter which vessel pours out the praise.

Where do you see competition at work in the church and Christian community?

How can a spirit of service and honor cancel out the spirit of competition?

Today, examine your heart. If you have been living in competition with a brother or sister in Christ, confess it to God and repent. Ask God to replace your attitude of competition with a spirit of service. Prayerfully choose one way you can serve and honor someone else this week.

DAY FOUR

BREAKING THE PATTERN TRAP

The warm, humid air enveloped us as we walked down the curving path through the butterfly house. Butterflies and moths flitted around our heads, pausing to drink from the jewel-bright flowers. A blue butterfly the size of my hand fluttered over, landing delicately on the sleeve of my lace sweater. I laughed and held still so I wouldn't startle it away. The butterfly rested for a moment, giving me a good look at the tiny scales that formed its intricate pattern. It fluttered as if trying to take off, but it stayed attached to my sweater. It beat its wings again as if struggling. I took a closer look. The butterfly's fragile legs had become entangled in the threads of my sweater. It was trapped.

Eventually a butterfly keeper was able to carefully untangle the butterfly from my sweater, setting it free. The experience made me think about how easy it is for us to become entangled and how hard it can be to free ourselves. Like the butterfly trapped in the threads of my sweater, we can become trapped and entangled by sin. Sometimes our own sin can trap us. And sometimes, like Leah, we can become trapped and entangled in sinful patterns that make it very difficult to break free.

We've seen that Leah was trapped in a pattern of competition with her sister. Yet Leah was also part of a dysfunctional family system whose patterns repeated from generation to generation.

Leah's husband, Jacob, was the son of Isaac and Rebekah. Isaac favored his older son, Esau. Rebekah favored Jacob. Their parents' favoritism led to conflict between Jacob and Esau much like there was between Rachel and Leah. As we've already seen, Jacob was also a deceiver who lied to his blind father. Eventually Jacob's deceit and conflict with his brother forced him to leave his home.

After leaving home, Jacob came face to face with a man who was a greater deceiver than he was: Leah and Rachel's father, Laban. Laban tricked Jacob into marrying Leah instead of Rachel, then manipulated Jacob into working for him for fourteen years so he could marry Rachel as well. Laban tried to cheat Jacob by changing his wages. Instead of keeping his daughters' bride prices safe to ensure their financial security, Laban treated this money as his own and devoured it. Laban's treachery eventually led Jacob and his family to deceive Laban and flee back to Canaan.

You would think that Jacob would have learned something about the danger of favoritism and conflict between siblings, but Jacob repeated the mistakes of his father. Jacob should have favored Leah's oldest son, Reuben, as the firstborn and chosen heir. Instead, Jacob favored Rachel's son, Joseph, the second youngest of his twelve sons. This favoritism led to resentment and anger among Jacob's older sons. Their resentment festered until it exploded. Jacob's older sons took Joseph captive, threw him into a cistern, and sold him as a slave. Then they took his cloak, covered it with blood, and told their father Joseph had been killed by a wild animal. Jacob had deceived his father, and now his sons deceived him.

Scripture is silent about Leah's thoughts and feelings regarding her family. We might look at this mess of lying, violent people and wonder how God choose or used any of them. Yet God's hand was all over this story. God eventually gave Jacob a new name: Israel. His twelve sons became the forefathers of Israel's twelve tribes. The thread of redemption ran through Leah's family—and it runs through yours.

Some of you reading this today come from messy families much like Leah's. Looking back at your family history reveals patterns of addiction, abuse, divorce, deceit, failure, and more. You might look at the brokenness and mess you come from and wonder how God could ever use you. Like a butterfly tangled in thread, you feel trapped by the patterns others have laid down for you. Yet God gives us hope.

📖 Read Ezekiel 18:19–23

Why does God say a son does not share his father's guilt?

What happens if a wicked person turns away from their sins?

According to this passage, what does God say pleases Him?

How does this give you hope?

We may have learned patterns of behavior from our families. Yet just because those before us failed to live faithfully before God does not doom us to repeat their mistakes. God holds us accountable for our own choices, and by the grace of God we can choose a different pattern.

📖 Read Romans 12:1–2.

To what pattern should we not conform?

What transforms us into a new pattern?

What is the result of this transformation?

Our experiences shape us, but they don't have to harden us. When we look at the patterns around us, we can choose to conform to those patterns or to let ourselves be transformed by the renewing of our minds. Changing our thinking changes our doing. The best way to change our thinking is to soak ourselves in Scripture so that we learn to think as God thinks, conforming ourselves to Christ's image.

This transformation may require us to learn new ways of thinking, speaking, and relating to others. These lessons may be hard, especially if we come from families who lived according to different patterns. But we can choose to conform ourselves to the pattern given us by the family of God.

📖 Read Ephesians 2:19

Whose household are you now a part of?

We have been adopted into God's family, with God as our Father, Christ as our elder brother, and all the saints of God standing as witnesses. Our identity has been changed, and now we live according to the pattern of this new family.

In the family of God:

We live at peace with one another (Mark 9:50)

We don't complain or grumble against each other (John 6:43; Galatians 5:26).

We forgive each other (Colossians 3:13)

We seek one another's good (1 Thessalonians 3:13).

We confess our sins to each other (James 5:16).

We serve one another (Galatians 3:13).

We honor one another, regarding them as more important than ourselves (Romans 12:10; Philippians 2:3).

We speak truth to one another (Ephesians 4:25).

We stimulate each other to love and good deeds (Hebrews 10:24)

We show hospitality to one another (1 Peter 4:9).

We encourage each other and build one another up (1 Thessalonians 5:11).

Which of these patterns of God's family comes most naturally to you?

_____

_____

Which of these patterns might require you to make changes to live according to it?

_____

_____

Prayerfully reflect on the patterns that have shaped your life. Which of these patterns do you want to keep? Which patterns do you need to be transformed by God's grace? As you identify unhealthy patterns that need change, seek out what God's Word has to say about them. Transform these patterns with the truth and thank God for making you a member of His family.

DAY FIVE

GOD'S GLORIOUS GRACE

Leah's home life and family were a mess. She was regarded as unlovely and unloved by her family. Yet God wove Leah into His tapestry of grace.

It's a pattern we see often in Scripture. God chooses the outsider, the foreigner, the younger sibling, the one others reject and overlook. Our weaknesses and frailties reveal God's grace.

So it was with Leah.

Leah drops out of the narrative after Jacob and his family left for Canaan. Rachel died giving birth to her second son and was buried along the way to Bethlehem. Scripture doesn't record Leah's grief over her sister's death, what she thought about her new home in Caanan, or if she lived long enough to see the turmoil between her sister's sons and hers. Through the rest of Genesis, Jacob only mentions Leah's name once more, when he tells his sons to bury him in the family tomb next to his forefathers—the same tomb where he had also buried Leah. The only other places Scripture records Leah's name are in genealogies. Even so those genealogies tell a story.

Read Genesis 35:23. What were the names of Leah's sons?

_____

Pay attention to two names in particular—Levi and Judah.

Jacob's family lived in Egypt for four hundred years, eventually growing into a nation and becoming slaves to Pharaoh. When God moved to free his people, He chose Moses, a member of the tribe of Levi, to be their deliverer. Moses' brother, Aaron, became Israel's first high priest. His sons became priests after him, and God chose the rest of the Levites to assist the priests and care for the tabernacle (Numbers 3:5–8).

📖 Read Deuteronomy 33:8–11.

This passage describes several of the main duties of a priest. Priests were to:

Know and discern God's will. The *Ummin* and *Thummin* were two carved stones the priests wore on their breastplate, or ephod. Old Testament law gave instructions for how the priests were to use the *Ummin* and *Thummin* to discern God's will.

Be loyal to God even above their own families. During the Exodus, there were times when the tribe of Levi had to deliver justice to those who had turned against God. The Levites had to administer justice even to members of their own families. This anticipates the redefining of loyalty we experience as believers.

Guard God's covenant and teach it to Israel. The priests were tasked with knowing God's law and teaching Israel how to obey it.

Worship God through sacrifice and offerings. The priests conducted the rituals of sacrifice and worship. They ministered before God in the tabernacle and offered sacrifices of worship, atonement, and thanksgiving to the Lord.

Represent God to the people and the people to God. The priests represented God to the people by helping them to know God's will and teaching them how to be obedient to God. They represented the people to God through intercession and through bringing sacrifices and offerings before the Lord.

What connections can you make between the responsibility of a priest and the responsibility of believers today?

Israel's priests trace their lineage back to Leah. Leah was also the mother of another prominent tribe: the tribe of Judah.

Read what Jacob prophesied about Judah in Genesis 49:10. What future did Jacob forsee for Judah's descendants?

Israel's kings eventually came from the line of Judah. Israel's first king, Saul, was from the tribe of Benjamin. Saul's sin led God to reject him as king. God chose David in his place. David was the son of Jesse, a member of the tribe of Judah.

📖 Read Deuteronomy 17:14–20. What were the responsibilities of Israel's king?

The kings of Israel were to serve God with undivided devotion. Instead of building up their security though military strength or marriage alliances, the kings of Israel were to trust God as their source of security. One of the king's chief responsibilities was to know the law by heart, writing out his own copy of the law and reading it all the days of his life. This knowledge of the law would help him revere God and live in obedience to the Lord. It would also serve as a check that would keep him from elevating himself above his fellow Israelites.

What similarities do you see between the responsibilities of the king and the responsibilities of believers today?

_____

_____

_____

David founded the ruling dynasty of Israel and Judah, but God also chose David as the forefather of another kingdom.

📖 Read God's promise to David in 2 Samuel 7:11–16. What did God promise David?

_____

_____

We know that eventually both Israel and Judah fell to foreign powers and were carried into exile. The reign of David's descendants seemed to come to an end. And yet, God's promise was not in vain. To understand how God kept His promise, we need to look to the New Testament.

📖 Read Luke 1:26–33. Who was Jesus descended from?

_____

How does this verse fulfill God's promise concerning the line of Judah?

_____

Jesus was the promised descendant of the line of Judah who reigns forever and has authority over all nations. His kingdom is secure. Our salvation comes from Him. And God wrote unloved, rejected, less-than Leah, smack dab into the middle of Jesus' family tree.

Leah became the mother of Israel's priests and kings. God chose her and wove a remarkable legacy from her life. This legacy speaks to us as well.

God chose Israel to be before Him a "kingdom of priests and a holy nation" (Exodus 19:6). All the earth belonged to the Lord, but God chose Israel to represent Him to the nations and the nations to God in the same way that Israel's priests served before the Lord. Their job was to be a holy nation that would point people to God.

As believers in Christ, we have the same commission.

📖 Read 1 Peter 2:9–10.

How are believers in God like priests?

_____

_____

How are we like kings?

_____

_____

For what purpose did God choose us as His special possession?

_____

_____

God chose us to receive His mercy and make a people from us: a people dedicated to His glory. As God's chosen people, we declare God's praises and honor. Like the priests, we represent God to the people through our witness. Through prayer and intercession, we represent the people to God. As citizens of God's kingdom and ambassadors of our Father, we extend the kingdom and reign of God on earth, seeing that God's will is done in and through us. Like the kings of Israel, we are to know God's covenant and laws so that we can lead others in obedience to God.

Leah's story encourages me in two ways. It reminds me that God has the final say over my story. God is the only one who gets to determine my value, and God has already said that I am priceless and precious to Him. So are you.

Leah's story also reminds me of both my identity and legacy. I am a part of God's royal priesthood. I am tasked with the responsibility of living out my obedience to God in a way that points people to Him. Being a member of God's kingdom means that I am tasked with being God's ambassador, both pleading with people to be reconciled to God and interceding for them before my Father.

This identity also belongs to you. You are a royal priest before the throne of God. Your witness points people to our Father, bringing glory to He who has shown us such great mercy. Even when we did not deserve it. Even when others said we were worthless. Even when our stories were messy and broken—God chose us and wove us into His story of salvation. You belong to Him.

NOTES

LESSON 6

GOMER

EMBRACING GOD'S REDEMPTION AND GRACE

DAY ONE

A LIVING PARABLE

Weddings are meant to be a time of joyful anticipation, and ours was no different—even if we managed to slightly rearrange the normal order of events: I bought my wedding dress and had the church booked before I was engaged. Heath and I had talked about getting married and had begun making plans, but he hadn't formally proposed when I came home the summer before our wedding. My mother and I looked at the calendar and realized that we needed to begin making arrangements. I was living halfway across the country, and I'd only be home one more time before our wedding date. By the time Heath actually pulled out the ring, we had wedding plans well underway. My family embraced Heath, and his family embraced me. We moved forward into our marriage, confident both in our love for each other and God's hand in bringing us together. Our wedding day was a bright new beginning of our lives coming together.

Hosea and Gomer's marriage had a very different beginning. Scripture introduces Hosea and Gomer's relationship this way:

> When the LORD began to speak through Hosea, the LORD said to him,
> "Go, marry a promiscuous woman and have children with her, for
> like an adulterous wife this land is guilty of unfaithfulness to the
> LORD." So he married Gomer daughter of Diblaim, and she conceived
> and bore him a son. (Hosea 1:2–3).

What unusual thing did God ask Hosea to do?

_____

_____

Why did God tell Hosea to take this course of action?

_____

_____

_____

Scripture tells us little about Gomer outside of her marriage to Hosea. She is identified only as the "daughter of Diblaim," a name not mentioned in Scripture outside of this passage. Outside of that brief mention of her family, the only other thing we know about her is her label: "a promiscuous woman."

Gomer's description as a promiscuous woman raises many questions for us. Some have suggested that she may have been a temple prostitute before her marriage, though I believe this to be unlikely. The Old Testament does include reference to temple prostitution, and we know prostitution and sexual rites were part of pagan worship elsewhere in the ancient Near East. However, it's not certain that temple prostitution was ever widespread within Israel, and the text does not clearly suggest that Gomer ever served in this manner.[11]

Others have suggested that perhaps Hosea married Gomer knowing that she would one day be unfaithful, but that she had not yet been unchaste. While possible, Scripture bluntly describes Gomer as a "promiscuous woman." The simplest reading is that Gomer had already proved herself to be unfaithful before Hosea married her.

Gomer's reputation is only one detail about her, but it is an important one. In ancient Israel, women were expected to be chaste prior to their marriage. A man who had sex with a virgin before marriage was required by law to pay her father the bride price and marry her. A woman who was found not to be a virgin at the time of her marriage was to be brought to the door of her father's house and stoned because "she has done an outrageous thing in Israel while being promiscuous while still in her father's house" (Deuteronomy 22:21).

Gomer was not put to death because of her promiscuity, but her reputation probably did not help her when it came time to find a husband. Few Israelite men would choose a woman who had slept with other men. What does it say about Gomer that in a culture where women's chastity was highly valued, she chose to break the moral and religious norms of her culture? Her actions showed that she was not overly concerned with God's commands or her own reputation. Perhaps she had a bit of a rebel streak. Perhaps she made choices she later regretted and couldn't figure out how to begin again. We don't know the hidden motivations of Gomer's heart, but it seems a logical assumption that Gomer was not devoted to the Lord.

We don't know what, if any, choice Gomer had in her marriage. Diblaim is not mentioned outside of his identity as Gomer's father. Perhaps he saw Gomer's marriage as an opportunity to get rid of his troublesome daughter. Maybe he hoped that a marriage would settle her down. Maybe he was simply willing to trade Gomer for the bride price Hosea offered. Again, we don't know. However, since Gomer was later unfaithful to Hosea and left him for another man, it seems likely that she did not walk into marriage with joyful anticipation. Hosea had her hand in marriage. He did not have her heart.

📖 We should not miss that God instructed Hosea to marry Gomer. Read Hosea 1:2 again:

When the LORD began to speak through Hosea, the LORD said to him,
"Go, marry a promiscuous woman and have children with her, for
like an adulterous wife this land is guilty of unfaithfulness to the
LORD."

What connection did God draw between Gomer's unfaithfulness and Israel's unfaithfulness?

God chose Hosea for a painful and powerful task. Through his marriage to an unfaithful woman, Hosea would demonstrate the compassion and faithfulness of God. His marriage would be a living parable. As Israel had been unfaithful to God, so Gomer would be unfaithful to Hosea. Hosea would provide a portrait of God's redeeming love.

DOCTRINE
Unequally Yoked

The New Testament says that a believer should not be "unequally yoked;" that is, a believer should not marry an unbeliever (2 Corinthians 6:14). Did Hosea disobey this command by marrying Gomer? No. For one thing, the New Testament had not been written when Hosea prophesied. While the Old Testament forbade Hebrew men from marrying women from some nations outside Israel (Deuteronomy 7:1–4), nothing in the Old Testament law forbade an Israelite man from marrying another Israelite woman. Hosea married Gomer in obedience to God's command, and the painful situation gave him an opportunity to demonstrate God's redeeming love.

Gomer, an unfaithful wife, was and is an illustration of Israel's unfaithfulness to God. Throughout Scripture, God uses marriage as a portrait of His relationship with His people.

Consider God's words through the prophet Isaiah:

For your Maker is your husband—

The LORD Almighty is his name—

The Holy One of Israel is your Redeemer,

He is called the God of all the earth" (Isaiah 54:5).

How is God's love for His people like that of a faithful husband?

God also compares His people's relationship with Him to that of a bride to her husband.

This is what the LORD says: I remember the devotion of your youth,
How as a bride you loved me
And followed me through the wilderness,
Through a land not sown (Jeremiah 2:2).

How was Israel's relationship with God like that of a bride to her husband?

_____

_____

Though God had promised His faithfulness to Israel, the people of Israel failed to live up to their faithful commitment to God.

📖 Read Hosea 4:1–12. List some of the ways in which the people of Israel demonstrated their unfaithfulness to God.

_____

_____

_____

It's important to remember that Israel's unfaithfulness was not a surprise to God. God's foreknowledge meant that when He redeemed Israel from their slavery in Egypt, He knew Israel would fail to live up to their commitment to Him. He knew that only weeks after their deliverance, Israel would build a golden calf in the desert and praise the statue their hands had made for delivering them out of Egypt (Exodus 32:7–8). God knew that they would turn back at the Jordan River. He knew that they would reject God's sovereignty over them and demand a king. He knew that they would chase after the gods of the nations around them, even sacrificing their own children to the fires of pagan gods. Just like Hosea married Gomer knowing that she would be unfaithful to him, God chose Israel with full foreknowledge of their unfaithfulness. In the same way, God also chose us despite being fully aware of every time we would sin against Him, betray Him, and reject His rightful Lordship over our lives. Revelation 13:8 describes Jesus as the Lamb of God "who was slain from the creation of the world." Before God spoke us into existence, He knew the price that would be paid for our redemption. Jesus paid it willingly.

📖 Read Romans 5:8 below:

But God demonstrates his own love for us in this: While we were still
sinners, Christ died for us.

What were we when Christ died for us? How does this demonstrate God's love?

_____

_____

Like Gomer's unfaithfulness to Hosea before her marriage, we have all demonstrated our unfaithfulness to God. Whether we sin by outright rebellion against God or by simply neglecting to do that which we know is right, all sin is a failure to give God the loyalty and undivided devotion He is properly due. Romans 3:23 says that "all have sinned and fall short of the glory of God." *All* means *all*. You. Me. All of us.

Gomer sinned in a very public way—a way that brought shame on her, to her family, to her husband, and to her children. As we'll see later this week, the consequences of her actions brought pain to her and to Hosea. Yet God also chose her to play a starring role in His great story of redemption. Gomer sinned greatly. But let us not remember her because of her great sin. Let us remember her because she was greatly redeemed.

Greatly redeemed. That's the message I'd like you to hold on to today. I don't know where this lesson finds you. Maybe, like Gomer, you have very public, painful sins from your past. Stains you'd like to erase. Choices you'd like to undo. Romans 5:8 is still true for you. *While you were still a sinner, Christ died for you.*

Maybe you don't identify with Gomer, but you carry the burden of your own set of failures and mistakes. You've committed sins that are more culturally acceptable, but still spiritually deadly. You carry the memory of words you'd like to unsay, grudges you can't get past, habits and failures that trip you up over and over again. Guilt is a companion, and you feel unworthy of God's love. Hear this: *While you were still a sinner, Christ died for you.*

This is the miracle: all have sinned and none of us are worthy. Christ loved us anyway. Like Hosea choosing Gomer despite her promiscuity and unfaithfulness, God chose us out of the mire of our failures, sins, and mistakes. We didn't love Him, but He loved us anyway. We didn't choose Him, but He chose us. We stand before God not because we deserve it, but because God gave us grace. We share one important part of Gomer's story: We too have been redeemed.

DAY TWO

A NEW NAME

We saw yesterday that Gomer had a reputation for promiscuity before her marriage to Hosea. Gomer's marriage might have offered her a chance for a new beginning. Sadly though, Gomer continued in the same patterns she had formed before her marriage. Though she was married to Hosea, Gomer continued to pursue relationships with other men. God had told Hosea to marry Gomer as an enacted parable of Israel's relationship with God, and her continued infidelity was a portrait of how Israel had abandoned the Lord.

Sin has consequences. Israel's abandonment of God introduced a breach in their relationship with God and a withdrawal of God's protection over the nation. Similarly, Gomer's unfaithfulness to Hosea introduced pain and brokenness into their relationship. Sadly,

Gomer's sin also affected her children. Gomer had three children while she was married to Hosea. The names of her children testify to the relationship between Israel and God.

IN THEIR SHOES
When God Doesn't Tell Us Why

Many have wondered why God would ask Hosea to do something that would cause him and his family such pain and suffering. Scripture never gives us a clear answer beyond the prophetic symbolism of Hosea's actions. Yet Hosea was not the only person in Scripture who might have wanted to ask God, "Why?" Why, when Paul was faithfully preaching the gospel, would God ask him to endure beatings, shipwreck, imprisonment, and eventually death? If God was going to give Abraham a son, why allow him and Sarah to experience the years of sorrow and grief over their infertility? Why allow Job to experience the loss of his possessions, family, and health? Why would God ask and allow faithful people to walk journeys of suffering and pain?

More often than not, we don't get the answer to our whys. And while in Scripture we can see God's hand at work and know the redemption at the end of the story, we can sometimes forget about the pain and confusion that the people who lived through the middle of those stories may have experienced—pain and confusion that may be much like what we experience when we live through our own why moments. On this side of heaven, we may not get the answers to why God allows what He allows. Yet in the middle of our pain and sorrow, God is faithful to remind us of who He is. Hosea experienced God's faithfulness in the midst of his pain, and God brought redemption to Hosea's story. If we can trust God with our own unanswered questions, God can remind us of the truth of who He is in the messy middles of our own stories. The God who brought redemption to Hosea's story can bring redemption to our stories, too.

Hosea named Gomer's first child Jezreel:

> *So he married Gomer, daughter of Diblaim, and she conceived and bore him a son. Then the Lord said to Hosea, "Call him Jezreel, because I will soon punish the house of Jehu for the massacre at Jezreel, and I will put an end to the kingdom of Israel. In that day I will break Israel's bow in the Valley of Jezreel." (Hosea 1:3–5)*

DID YOU KNOW?
Israel's Bow

A bow was a symbol of military strength. When God said that He would "break Israel's bow" (Hosea 1:3) He was promising to break Israel's military power. Israel's broken covenant with God would lead to a withdrawal of God's protection and its eventual military defeat.

Jezreel was the location of one of the greatest acts of violence in Israel's history. God appointed Jehu king over Israel, but Jehu set about securing his throne through a massacre. He killed King Joram, who had become king after King Ahab. Jehu also killed Jezebel, Ahab's wife and Joram's mother, seventy sons of Ahab, and many of Ahab's advisors and court officials. In the midst of this bloody purge, forty-two members of Judah's royal family came to visit Joram and Jezebel. Jehu killed them as well, beginning his reign with a bloodbath. By naming his son Jezreel, Hosea recalled this great slaughter in Israel's history and anticipated the greater slaughter that would come when Assyria invaded Israel.

EXTRA MILE
Israel's Bow

You can read about Jehu and the slaughter at Jezreel in 2 Kings 9:14–37.

Jezreel's name was both an indictment of Israel's past and a prediction of the judgment to come in Israel's future. The names of Gomer's other children followed similar patterns.

📖 Read Hosea 1:6–7.

What was Gomer's daughter's name?

_____

What did her name mean?

_____

Why did God tell Hosea to give her this name?

_____

_____

Interestingly, the wording is slightly different in the announcement of Gomer's second child's birth. The Bible says that "Gomer . . conceived and bore [Hosea] a son" when it announces Jezreel's birth. However, it announces Lo-Ruhamah's birth as "Gomer conceived again and gave birth to a daughter." It says that Gomer bore a daughter—not that she bore a child to Hosea. The implication may be that Lo-Ruhamah was Gomer's child but not Hosea's. If so, Gomer's infidelity to Hosea had already begun.

Lo-Ruhamah's name was a sign that Israel's unfaithfulness had separated Israel from God. We know that God does not stop loving us, but our sin can prevent us from experiencing and understanding His love because our sin separates us from Him.

How have you seen sin separate you from God?

_____

_____

_____

What hope is there for us when sin prevents us from experiencing God's love?

_____

Scripture also announces the birth of Gomer's third child in a way that implies this child may not have been Hosea's either.

📖 Read Hosea 1:8-9.

What was the name of Gomer's third child? What did this name mean?

_____

_____

What might have caused God to say that Israel was not His people and He was not their God?

_____

_____

To be clear, God was not the one who had abandoned Israel. By pursuing idols and breaking their covenant, Israel had rejected God. Israel's idol worship declared that they were no longer God's people and He was no longer their God. In this pronouncement of judgment, God was declaring the effect of decisions Israel had already made. God had not rejected His people. His people had rejected Him.

Scripture doesn't tell us what Gomer thought about the names Hosea gave her children. Did she shrug it off as unimportant? Or did it break her heart every time she called them to the dinner table? Did the labels given to her children feel like additional weight on the labels she already bore? _Promiscuous. Unfaithful. Rejected. Unloved._ Yet whenever God pronounces judgment, He also pronounces restoration and hope. Just as the names of Gomer's children illustrated Israel's rejection of God, they also pointed to God's redemption of Israel. Perhaps one day Gomer also understood how they gave hope for her redemption.

📖 Read Hosea 1:10-11 and 2:15-25

What hope do these verses give to Israel?

_____

_____

How do they reverse the names of judgment given to Hosea's children?

_____

_____

God looked forward to a day when Israel would return to God in faithfulness. On that day Israel would no longer serve God as a slave serves his or her master. Instead, Israel would pledge her loving faithfulness to the Lord as a bride to her husband. God would respond to Israel's repentance. Instead of uprooting them from the land in exile, God would plant and settle His people. Those called "Not my loved one" would experience God's redeeming love, and those called "not my people" would become a people for God's own possession (Hosea 2:23). The places in Israel's past that had been memorials to their past disobedience would become doors to future hope (Hosea 2:15).

DID YOU KNOW?
The Valley of Achor

Hosea 2:15 says that God would make the "Valley of Achor a door of hope." The Valley of Achor marked the place where Achan was stoned after he disobeyed God's command and took plunder from the city of Jericho (Joshua 7). Achan's disobedience led to defeat for Israel. God promised to take that place of disobedience and judgment and transform it into a door of hope.

Sometimes we bear the names others have given us. Unloved. Not belonging. Stupid. Fat. Not worthy. We can hear these names so much that we begin to use them to name ourselves. *Guilty. Shameful. Rejected. Failure.* Our sin separates us from God, and Satan begins to whisper to us that the isolation we know now is all we deserve and all our lives will ever be. Yet God has given us a new name.

> *Whoever has ears, let them hear what the Spirit says to the churches.*
> *To the one who is victorious, I will give some of the hidden manna. I*
> *will also give that person a white stone with a new name written on*
> *it, known only to the one who receives it. (Revelation 2:17)*

DID YOU KNOW?
White Stones

White stones (mentioned in Revelation 2:17) were connected with a "not guilty" verdict in court as well as admission to a feast or a guild. In the context of this passage the stone may be a symbol of forgiveness and acceptance, showing that God has declared us innocent and invited us to enter His kingdom.

Our sin separates us from God, but Jesus' blood reconciles us to Him. When we repent and accept Christ's forgiveness, God restores us and gives us a new name—a name that signifies our relationship with Him.

People may have said you were not loved. God loved you enough to send Jesus.

People may have said you were not one of them. God says you belong to Him.

People said your life was irrevocably scarred by violence and suffering. God takes those broken places in your lives and transforms them into a door of hope.

People said your sin built a wall between you and God. God tore it down. Where the wall once stood, the cross now beckons you home.

What names or labels have others put on you? What new name does God want to give you in their place?

_____

_____

_____

Your past may have shaped you, but God gets to define your future. It's time to take off the labels. Embrace the new name God has given you—a name that gives you a future and a hope: His.

DAY THREE

BORN TO RUN

My childhood dog was a beagle and dachshund mix with white fur almost the same shade as my light blond hair. I named her Blondie. She was a good dog for a little girl, but Blondie had a fatal flaw: she was born to wander. Most of the time she lived contentedly within the confines of our home and yard. But as soon as she saw an open gate or a cracked door, all bets were off: Blondie was on the run. When the scent of freedom was in the air, she refused to respond to my frantic calls. All she would do was run, and there was no catching her. Eventually she'd wear herself out, calm down, and come home.

Blondie was my dog, but she had a little of my spirit as well. I've lived the good girl life, but I recognize I have a streak in my spirit that (as the hymn aptly describes) is "prone to wander" and "prone to leave the God I love."[12] The daylight beyond that open gate shines bright. Like Blondie, when temptation hits, I'm born to run. Running feels good for a moment, but those seductive temptations that seem so promising turn to ashes in my hands.

That's where I identify with Gomer's story. Like Gomer, I don't always understand that boundaries are protection, not prison. I forget that my truest freedom is found in the confines of God's grace. I chase after the things that lure me away from my fidelity to Christ, and chasing the illusion of freedom leaves me trapped and enslaved.

It's easy for us to sit in judgment on Gomer. She was unfaithful to her husband! Left her children! Wound up another man's slave! Yet we need to be honest about the unfaithfulness of our own hearts. Gomer's unfaithfulness to Hosea was a portrait of Israel's unfaithfulness to God. If God's own people could be unfaithful to Him, so can we. If we don't want to follow in Gomer's footsteps, we need to recognize our own propensity to wander from the God we love. What leads us astray? And how do we battle that temptation? Gomer's story doesn't have to be ours. We can find victory over sin. Scripture tells us how.

First, we need to recognize the true source of temptation. When we're tempted, it's easy to turn to blame. It's a story as old as creation. God gave Adam and Eve one prohibition: do not eat from the tree of the knowledge of good and evil. Satan tempted Eve to eat from the tree anyway. Eve looked, saw that the fruit looked good, took it, ate it, and gave some to Adam. When God confronted them, Adam blamed both God and Eve. "It was the woman you gave me." Eve blamed the serpent. Too often that trick is still our go-to plan. "God let me be tempted beyond what I could take." "Satan made me do it." "They did it first." The truth is that God doesn't tempt us. Satan, for all his lying ways, has no power to make us do anything, and other people's sin does not excuse our own. What does have the power to lead us astray?

📖 Read James 1:13–15:

> *When tempted, no one should say, "God is tempting me." For God cannot be tempted by evil, nor does he tempt anyone; but each person is tempted when they are dragged away by their own evil desire and enticed. Then, after desire has conceived, it gives birth to sin; and sin, when it is full-grown, gives birth to death.*

How do we know that God does not tempt us?

What does tempt us?

What are the results of this temptation?

We must come to grips with the fact that our own desires entice us into sin. We want the wrong things—or sometimes we want the right things in the wrong way. Once conceived in our minds and hearts, our sinful desires give birth to sinful action. That sin, once planted in our lives, yields death.

We want revenge, so we give in to bitterness and backstabbing.

We want distraction, so we procrastinate, consume media unthinkingly, and fritter away time.

We want satisfaction, so we gorge ourselves on shopping, unhealthy foods, or mindless entertainment.

We want intimacy, so we turn to erotica and porn.

We want to belong, so we create the illusion of community with outrage, gossip, and complaining.

We want security, so we try to buy it with our bank accounts or votes.

We want wisdom, so we chase gurus with slick sounding words or go down the rabbit hole of internet conspiracies, convincing ourselves we are the only ones with true knowledge.

Pause for a moment and consider what you desire. Not the surface level desires of losing a few pounds, chocolate, or the new flooring for your kitchen. Cut down to the bone. At your core, in the marrow of your bones, what do you want? What do you crave?

What are your desires?

How could those desires lead you astray?

How could you reshape those desires to point you to God?

Our desires can lead us into sin. But God also gives us hope. Because of what Christ has done for us, we do not have to fall into temptation. We can stand firm.

📖 Read 1 Corinthians 10:12–13:

> *So, if you think you are standing firm, be careful that you don't fall. No temptation has overtaken you except what is common to mankind. And God is faithful; he will not let you be tempted beyond what you can bear. But when you are tempted, he will also provide a way out so that you can endure it.*

If we think we are standing firm, what do we need to be careful about? Why?

_____

_____

_____

How does this passage encourage you when you face temptation?

_____

_____

_____

One of the powerful truths in this passage is that we are not alone in our temptations. When we are tempted, Satan often tries to isolate us with his lies, making us believe that we are alone, that no one else is tempted by this as we are, and that we should be ashamed of ourselves for being so weak. These are lies. "No temptation has overtaken you except what is common to mankind." Our temptations are common. Others share them with us as Christ has also shared them. If we are willing to take the risk about our struggles, we can break the bonds of isolation and encourage one another. Secrets lose their power when they are shared. Confessing our sins to one another helps us find victory and gives us strength.

IN THEIR SHOES
One Tempted as We Are

Jesus can understand our temptations because He was also tempted, but He did not yield to sin. "For we do not have a high priest who is unable to empathize with our weaknesses, but we have one who has been tempted in every way, just as we are—yet He did not sin." (Hebrews 4:15)

These verses also remind us of God's faithfulness. When we face temptation, we have a choice. God will not let us be tempted beyond what we can bear. In His grace, God leaves us an escape route. We can leave the conversation, turn off the computer, and cut up the credit card. We can set aside unhealthy patterns and train ourselves in the way of faithfulness. Because the same power that raised Christ from the dead lives in us, we now have the freedom not to sin. We can choose faithfulness. We can choose to resist temptation. Satan has no more power over us, and we can find the way out God has provided for us.

The Spirit of him who raised Jesus from the dead is living in you.
(Romans 8:11)

Consider the temptations you battle on a daily basis. What are some of the ways God has provided for you to escape that temptation?

How does it help you to know that you are not alone in your battle against temptation? Who could you share your struggles with and ask to pray for you?

Today, know that Gomer's story does not have to be yours. Perhaps, like mine, your heart is prone to wander. We can conquer our wandering hearts, resist temptation, and bind ourselves to Christ. Temptation is real. Our desires entice us. But God always leaves a way of escape if we will only look for it. Close out today by praying the next line of the old hymn: "Here's my heart Lord, take and seal it. Seal it for thy courts above."[13]

DAY FOUR

REDEEMED

Some nights I wish God had never invented 3:00 a.m. I wake up and lie there staring at the unrelenting glow of the numbers on the alarm clock. Like a perpetual motion machine, my mind insists on replaying all the things I don't want to remember. Times I failed or looked foolish. When I reacted in anger instead of responding with love. When I remained silent instead of speaking the needed words of truth. When I indulged myself instead of doing the long hard work of discipline. Though I know I don't need to be perfect, in those 3:00 a.m. moments it can be hard to make my heart believe it. It's in those moments I need to remember the power of God's unfailing grace.

My tendency is to beat myself up over my lack of perfection. Other people respond to their inability to be perfect by refusing to try. Gomer seems to have been wired this way.

Prone to rebellion, not concerned with other people's opinions, determined to be who she was rather than trying and failing to live up to an ideal she felt she could never achieve. Perhaps it was this that made her unreceptive to God's offer of grace that came through her marriage to Hosea. Instead of using the opportunity for a new beginning, Gomer refused to try. She continued in her patterns of adultery and unfaithfulness. Eventually she left Hosea for another man and became his slave.

Hosea would have had every reason to give up on Gomer. She had repeatedly been unfaithful to him. She had abandoned him and her children, completely giving herself to another man. Whether by another's deceit or her own folly, Gomer had become another man's slave. Hosea was within his rights to divorce her and end the marriage. God commanded Hosea to do something radically different.

📖 Read Hosea 3:1–5.

How did God tell Hosea to treat Gomer?

What did Hosea do?

Hosea could have given up on Gomer, leaving her to the consequences of the choices she had made. Instead he redeemed her. By purchasing Gomer back from her slavery, Hosea gives us a portrait of God's unfailing, unshakable grace.

How is Hosea's treatment of Gomer like God's treatment of us?

God would have every reason to abandon us and leave us in our sin. God created us to honor and worship Him, yet we have all rejected Him. Justice dictates God should give us the punishment for our sins we deserve: death and separation from God. But God, in His great compassion and mercy, sent Jesus to take the penalty for us. Jesus's death paid the price for our sins, purchasing us back from sin's slavery. Like Gomer, we have been redeemed. Paul describes our redemption this way:

> *All have sinned and fall short of the glory of God, and all are justified freely by his grace through the redemption that came by Christ Jesus. God presented Christ as a sacrifice of atonement, through the shedding of his blood—to be received by faith. (Romans 3:23–25)*

To be redeemed is to be bought back from or purchased out of slavery. Just as Hosea redeemed Gomer from the slavery her sin had trapped her in, God purchased us from the slavery of our own sin. Christ's blood both atoned for—canceled the judgment for our sin—and redeemed us by purchasing our freedom from sin's slavery.

DOCTRINE
Atonement and Redemption

Atonement describes the reconciliation between God and humanity made possible by Christ's sacrifice. *Redemption* describes being bought back from or purchased out of slavery.

Gomer is not mentioned again in Scripture after Hosea chapter 3. We don't know how her story ended after Hosea brought her home. Did she change her life or go back to her old ways? Did she learn to receive the great gift she had been given—not only of her husband's love but of God's unfailing grace?

We don't know how Gomer's story ended, but there's another story in Scripture that reminds me of how I hope her story ended.

📖 Read Luke 7:36–50.

How does the woman in this story remind you of Gomer?

_____

_____

Like Gomer, the woman in this story had a reputation. She was a "sinful woman." The Pharisees with whom Jesus ate didn't think she belonged among the respectable people of the community—certainly not performing the intimate service of washing Jesus' feet. Yet her willingness to humble herself before Jesus demonstrates the depth of her gratitude. She had encountered God's forgiveness and grace, and so she gave up her most priceless possession in an act of extravagant worship.

Jesus's words to Simon echo the redemption I hope Gomer found:

> *I tell you her many sins are forgiven—as her great love has shown.*
> *But whoever has been forgiven little loves little (Luke 7:47).*

Like Gomer, this woman had greatly sinned. But being forgiven greatly prompted her to greatly love. We don't know how she met Jesus, but we know that she realized the depths of her sin were overwhelmed by the riches of God's forgiveness and grace. She responded to God's great forgiveness with gratitude that showed the greatness of her love.

I hope Gomer found a similar place in God's story of salvation—that she too discovered that those who are forgiven greatly love greatly. And this is the miracle: we've all been forgiven greatly.

That's the truth that stills my running thoughts and brings me peace on those wakeful 3:00 a.m. nights. *I have been forgiven greatly.* Like Gomer. Like Israel. Like the woman with the alabaster jar. Like you. Jesus's death paid it all. Whatever mistakes I've made, whatever bondage I've sold myself into, Jesus's death paid the price for my redemption. I am redeemed. How else can I respond but with extravagant worship and grateful love?

Today, thank God for the miracle of your redemption. Write out a prayer below thanking God for His unfailing, unchanging love.

DAY FIVE

THE FAITHFUL BRIDE

I mentioned earlier in this lesson about my wedding planning and a little about the wedding itself and the early days of my marriage. I remember I woke up early on my wedding day. The hair stylist who had done my hair since middle school opened up his shop just for me that morning. My mom and two of my best friends helped me step into the big white dress with the flowing train. The florist brought the bouquet, and we wove the string of my grandmother's pearls through it. We'd spent months preparing, and now it was time for our new lives to begin.

Weddings are marked by anticipation and preparation. Though the customs are different, we share the anticipation and preparation of marriage with brides and grooms from Jesus's time. The bride and groom were legally bound once the betrothal contract was signed, but the marriage did not take place until the wedding day. The groom would go to prepare a place for his bride and then return for her. The marriage only took place once the groom returned to claim his bride, and only then did the bride and groom begin their lives together.

Jesus often used this image to explain His relationship to His church. The betrothal document has been signed. Jesus claimed us on the cross. Yet the day of consummation has not yet come. We wait in anticipation and preparation for Christ's return. When he comes for us, a new era will begin, and God will be fully present with His people.

Gomer had her own wedding ceremony, but she did not pledge herself to Hosea in faithfulness. Although I have hopes for how her story ended, Scripture leaves Gomer's story unfinished. Scripture is silent about the outcome of Gomer's marriage, but it speaks loudly about our destiny as the bride of Christ.

As Christ's bride, we live in a season of anticipation and preparation as we wait for His certain coming. We do not know the day of Christ's coming, but we do know that He will surely come. Gomer did not live out her commitment to Hosea, but we can fulfill our commitment to Christ. Yet it is not enough for us to simply vow to resist temptation. To remain faithful, we must cultivate faithfulness. One day, God's dwelling place will be with us. We prepare ourselves for that glorious future now.

Like a bride waiting for her groom, we can be certain of Christ's return. Our confidence in His return should motivate our obedience today.

📖 Read Revelation 21:1–4.

How certain are you of Christ's coming?

_____

_____

_____

How does your knowledge that Christ will one day return impact your life today?

_____

_____

_____

The apostle Peter said this about how we should prepare ourselves for Christ's coming:

> *But then in keeping with his promise we are looking forward to a*
> *new heaven and a new earth, where righteousness dwells. So then,*
> *dear friends, since you are looking forward to this, make every effort*
> *to be found spotless, blameless, and at peace with him. (2 Peter*
> *3:13–14)*

What are we anticipating?

_____

_____

How should this anticipation motivate us to be prepared? How much effort should we put into this preparation?

_____

_____

The idea of being spotless and blameless connects back with images from the Old Testament. The Passover celebrated how God freed the Hebrew people from slavery in Egypt. The centerpiece of this memorial was the sacrifice of the Passover Lamb. This sacrificial lamb had to be perfect, without any spot or blemish. The New Testament draws on this imagery by calling Jesus the "Lamb of God." As the blood of the Passover lamb marked the homes of God's people and spared them God's judgment, so Christ's blood marks us and spares us the judgment for our sins. Peter called Christ "a lamb without blemish or defect" (1 Peter 1:19). For us to live spotlessly and blamelessly means that we are to reflect the very character of Christ.

We become what we worship. If we worship the worthless idols of our own making, we become as ineffectual and powerless as a statue of stone.[14] But if we worship Christ, we become like Christ: righteous and holy. Christ faced temptation, but He lived without sin. As we grow in relationship to Christ, we come to reflect His spotless and blameless character.

Living at peace with God is a benefit of our relationship with Christ. God is eternally opposed to sin. All sin—including our own. Christ's death ended that conflict and reconciled us to God. We now live at peace with God, enjoying the benefits of our relationship with Him.

This transformation into Christ's image does not happen by itself. The Holy Spirit is at work in us, but we must daily make the choice to turn from our sin and live toward God.

As God spoke to the people of Israel through Hosea, He gave them this instruction for how they were to return to Him.

> *You must return to your God; maintain love and justice, and wait for your God always. (Hosea 12:6)*

This verse echoes the words of the prophet Micah:

> *He has shown you, O mortal, what is good. And what does the LORD require of you? To act justly and to love mercy and to walk humbly with your God. (Micah 6:8)*

What do these verses express about what God expects of us?

How are you living up to those expectations?

Living in obedience to Christ means putting God's commands to work in our lives. This requires our active participation. It's not enough to hope to live like Jesus. Day by day, moment by moment, we must make the choices that turn us away from our sin and orient us toward God. We say yes to love, to peace, to justice, to mercy. In order to say yes to those things, we must say no to our own selfishness, pride, passivity, and anger. We do these things so we will be found ready on the day of Christ's return—spotless, blameless, and at peace with God.

CONCLUSION

The daughters of Zelophehad.

Abigail.

Huldah.

The widow of Zarephath.

Leah.

Gomer.

Their stories in Scripture are brief. Some are unnamed. Some give us only glimpses of their stories, leaving us with imaginings and unanswered questions. Yet God wove them into His great story of salvation history. They speak to us of God's heart for the marginalized, of the magnitude of the inheritance we have in Christ, of the importance of clinging to God's Word, of God's power to transform our brokenness, and of the depth and breadth of God's redemption. God says that their stories are worthy of remembrance, and they are part of the great cloud of witnesses cheering us on as we walk out this journey of faith.

You are significant. When the weight of the everyday presses down on us, it's easy to forget that simple truth. Yet truth remains. You are created in the image of God, a person Christ died for, a woman with a divinely-ordained purpose God has given you. Step forward. Let the daughters of Zelophehad give you the courage to claim your spiritual inheritance. May Abigail remind of the power of wisdom and prudence. Like Huldah, devote yourself to Scripture and don't flinch from declaring its uncompromising truth. Like the widow of Zarephath, God has sought after you. Like Leah, He has declared you chosen and beloved. And like Gomer, He has redeemed you. Serve the Lord faithfully. Worship God exclusively. Love Christ wholeheartedly. When you do, you will live life a worthy of remembrance. Like our sisters before us, you will leave a legacy that will be *unforgotten.*

Endnotes

1. David A. Aaron, "The Ruse of Zelophehad's Daughters" *Hebrew Union College Annual* 80 (2009): 1-38, http://www.jstor.org/stable/23509779; Mayer I., Gruber, *Israel Exploration Journal* 59, no. 1 (2009): 123–25, http://www.jstor.org/stable/27927221.

2. Dean R. Ulrich, "The Framing Function of the Narratives About Zelophehad's Daughters," *Journal of the Evangelical Theological Society* 41/4 (1998), 529-538.

3. James A. Meek, "The Riches of His Inheritance," *Presbyterion* 28, no. 1 (2002) 34–46, ATLASerials, Religion Collection, EBSCOhost (accessed June 26, 2018), (35).

4. *Ibid.*, 45.

5. Walter Brueggemann, *First and Second Samuel*, Interpretation (Louisville: Westminster John Knox Press, 1990), Kindle edition, Kindle Loc. 3431

6. Megan K. DeFranza, "The Proverbs 31 'Woman of Strength': An Argument for a Primary-Sense Translation," *Priscilla Papers* 25, no 1 (2011), 21–25, https://www.cbeinternational.org/sites/default/files/Proverbs_DeFranza.pdf.

7. "LifeWay Research: Americans Are Fond of the Bible, Don't Actually Read It," LifeWay Research, April 25, 2017, https://lifewayresearch.com/2017/04/25/lifeway-research-americans-are-fond-of-the-bible-dont-actually-read-it/

8. John Kuo, *Tempting Faith: An Inside Story of Political Seduction* (New York: Free Press, 2006, 172.

9. Ron Chernow, *Alexander Hamilton* (New York: Penguin Books, 2004), Kindle Edition.

10. "Assyrian Marriage Contract Contains Surrogacy Clause In Event of Infertility," Archeology News Network, November 10, 2017, https://archaeology-newsnetwork.blogspot.com/2017/11/assyrian-marriage-contract-contains.html

11. R. K. Harrison, *Introduction to the Old Testament* (Peabody, MA: Prince Press, 1999), 864.

12. Hymn, "Come Thou Fount of Many Blessings" by Robert Robinson, 1758.

13. *Ibid.*

14. G. K. Beale *We Become What We Worship: A Biblical Theology of Idolatry* (Downers Grove, IL: InterVarsity Press, 2008).

APPENDIX 1: HOW TO RECEIVE CHRIST

Agree with God about your sin.

For all have sinned and fall short of the glory or God. (Romans 3:23)

For the wages of sin is death. (Romans 6:23)

Believe that because of His great love for you, God sent Jesus, His one and only son, to die in your place and pay the price for your sins.

For God so loved the world that he gave his one and only Son, that whoever believes in him shall not perish but have eternal life. (John 3:16)

But God demonstrates his own love for us in this: While we were still sinners, Christ died for us. (Romans 5:8)

Admit to God that you have sinned and ask God for His forgiveness.

If we confess our sins, he is faithful and just and will forgive us our sins and purify us from all unrighteousness. (1 John 1:9)

Commit yourself to following Jesus as Lord, pledging your devotion, loyalty, and service to Him.

If you declare with your mouth "Jesus is Lord" and believe in your heart that God raised him from the dead, you will be saved. For it is with your heart that you believe and are justified, and it is with your mouth that you profess your faith and are saved. (Romans 10:9-10)

APPENDIX 2: IF YOU ARE A VICTIM OF VIOLENCE

If you are a victim of domestic violence, seek help. Physical, sexual, and emotional abuse are crimes. The following resources are places you can contact to seek help.

National Domestic Violence Hotline

1800-799-SAFE

www.thehotline.org

RAINN National Sexual Assault Hotline

800-656-HOPE

https://www.rainn.org/

The Global Network of Women's Shelters works to support, network, and provide information about women's shelters around the world. Find more information at their website: https://gnws.org/

The UN's Global Database of Violence against Women also maintains a list of international domestic violence hotlines and shelters. Search the database at their website: https://evaw-global-database.unwomen.org

WALKING HAND IN HAND AS CHRIST'S LOVE
transforms lives

AMG
INTERNATIONAL | MEETING THE **DEEPEST NEEDS**

WE BELIEVE THE GOSPEL IS TRANSFORMATIVE
And you can change the world one child at a time.

Thousands of children in the world are born into a cycle of poverty that has been around for generations, leaving them without hope for a safe and secure future. For a little more than $1 a day you can provide the tools a child needs to break the cycle in the name of Jesus.

OUR CONTACT

📞 423-894-6060
✉️ info@amginternational.org

📷 @amgintl
📍 6815 Shallowford Rd. Chattanooga, TN 37421

Made in the USA
Middletown, DE
11 March 2022

62399890R00071